UNDERSTANDING CHILDREN

An Interview and Observation Guide for Educators

UNDERSTANDING CHILDREN

An Interview and Observation Guide for Educators

Denise H. Daniels
California Polytechnic State University, San Luis Obispo

Lorrie J. Beaumont
Northern Illinois University

Carol A. Doolin
Northern Illinois University

Boston   Burr Ridge, IL   Dubuque, IA   Madison, WI   New York   San Francisco   St. Louis
Bangkok   Bogotá   Caracas   Kuala Lumpur   Lisbon   London   Madrid   Mexico City
Milan   Montreal   New Delhi   Santiago   Seoul   Singapore   Sydney   Taipei   Toronto

McGraw-Hill Higher Education

A Division of The McGraw-Hill Companies

UNDERSTANDING CHILDREN:
AN INTERVIEW AND OBSERVATION GUIDE FOR EDUCATORS

This book is printed on acid-free paper.

1 2 3 4 5 6 7 8 9 0 CUS/CUS 0 9 8 7 6 5 4 3 2 1

ISBN 0-07-248185-4

Editorial director: *Jane Karpacz*
Sponsoring editor: *Beth Kaufman*
Developmental editor: *Cara Harvey*
Senior marketing manager: *Daniel M. Loch*
Project manager: *Jean R. Starr*
Senior production supervisor: *Lori Koetters*
Senior Designer: *Jenny El-Shamy*
Cover design: *Adam Rooke*
Interior design: *Reuben Kantor*
Typeface: *ITC Garamond*
Compositor: *Reuben Kantor*
Printer: *Von Hoffmann Graphics, Inc.*

Library of Congress Control Number: 2001093932

www.mhhe.com

*To Derek and Leslie Daniels, Emily Durrell, Sarah and
Josh Beaumont and Jamie and Jennifer Doolin.
Thanks for all that you have taught us!*

About the Authors

Denise Daniels, Ph.D., is an associate professor of educational psychology with expertise in developmental studies. She has taught child development courses for educators for over ten years. Dr. Daniels investigates children's motivational processes, and uses interviews and observation to gain a more complete understanding of children's development in educational settings. She is committed to enhancing educators' understandings of child development through directed experiences observing and interviewing children.

Lorrie Beaumont is an evaluator of museum education programs, a former kindergarten teacher, and an instructor of child development classes for pre-service teachers. She also conducts workshops focused on interviewing and observing children. She believes strongly that children should have a voice in the development of the museum exhibits and programs with which they will participate. Likewise she believes that children should have a voice in their classroom experience and that educators need to become familiar with techniques that will help them get at the child's perspective.

Carol Doolin is a school psychologist, has had previous experience teaching in the elementary school classroom, and teaches university classes in child development and educational assessment. She feels that observation of children's behavior is a critical component in learning to understand children. A richer understanding of behavior is gained when examining the meaning children attribute to it in interviews.

Contents

List of Strategies

Preface

AN INTERVIEW AND OBSERVATION GUIDE FOR FUTURE EDUCATORS

Understanding Children: An Interview and Observation Guide for Educators was created to help future educators better understand children's behaviors and perspectives through the use of observations and interviews. It provides guidelines and means for conducting relevant, manageable observation and interview activities in classrooms and other educational settings, and can be adapted for use by teachers and other professionals studying child development. The specific observation and interview strategies are linked to developmental theories and research. The strategies should be considered as templates for child study students to test, adapt, and expand to meet their needs.

AUDIENCE

In general, the guide was written for pre-service educators to help them see how children develop across grade levels. However, the guide is also a valuable resource for non-educators studying child development, as well as for classroom teachers. For teachers, the strategies can help them better understand the students in their classrooms. All child study students are expected to benefit from connecting developmental theory and research to directed interview and observation experiences with real children.

We expect that child study students with varying levels of experience and knowledge will find this book useful. Some familiarity with theories and research in child development and terminology related to the observation and interview process is necessary for effective use of the strategies presented in the following chapters (i.e., students must have a reference child development text). Some child study students may be learning and practicing interview and observation skills for the first time while others may be using these strategies to further develop and strengthen the skills they already possess.

ORGANIZATION OF THE GUIDE

The topical organization of this guide is similar to formats used in many child development texts. However, the guide can be adapted for use in courses arranged chronologically. Whichever approach you are using, consult the *List of Strategies* on page xi for a full listing of the strategies.

The first chapter provides an introduction to the guide as well as to the importance of conducting child observations and interviews. Chapter 2 discusses the role of the child study student as an observer and an interviewer, introduces key observation and interview techniques, and discusses important ethical considerations.

Chapters 3–5 provide observation and interview strategies for studying children's development in the physical, cognitive, and social-emotional domains. Instructors should select those they feel would be most useful for their students. Each of these chapters includes a variety of strategies using different observation and interview approaches and theoretical perspectives. The strategies are preceded by contextual introductions, and concluded by an *Interpreting Observations and Interviews* section that provides hints for interpreting findings in light of some previous research. Concluding each of these chapters is *Tips for Teachers* — a feature that provides additional support for teachers interested in implementing observation and interview strategies in the classroom. *Reflection Questions* help the child study student connect observations and interview responses to theoretical and educational discussions.

Chapter 6 provides two child profiles as examples of how to integrate information gathered through observation and interview strategies presented in Chapters 3–5. These examples are presented to assist child study students with constructing student profiles or brief case studies, and teachers with building student files. Our aim is to encourage educators to regularly incorporate interview and observation strategies into their studies and classroom routines.

USING THE GUIDE

As a supplemental text, this guide should be used alongside a child development textbook. Readers are often referred to their child development text for assistance with planning as well as interpreting interviews and observations. While we cite background theory and research, particularly in cases where it may not be found in the primary text, it is not meant to be exhaustive.

The strategies suggested in this supplement are not for research nor diagnostic purposes. The main purpose for providing a guide such as this is to make child development research and theories come alive for those interested in studying children. Through guided authentic observational and interview experiences, students will become more familiar with children across grade levels, and better able to "see" evidence of their physical, cognitive, and socioemotional development. *Reflection Questions* located at the end of Chapters 3–5 encourage reflection on educational implications.

We recognize that in some child development courses, students have limited time for field experiences. Therefore, we offer the following suggestions:

1. Select a few strategies from Chapters 3–5 that seem the most appropriate for your particular course. Chapters 3–5 are arranged topically: physical development, cognitive development, and socio-emotional development.

2. Choose children from particular age groups or grade levels to interview and observe rather than the entire age range indicated. Many strategies in this text are

designed to reveal age-related differences (between 4 and 14 years) in behavior, thus a fairly wide range is suggested.

3. Arrange for student groups or teams to share the following responsibilities: a) gather and prepare materials; b) create operational definitions; c) interview and observe children from different age groups (e.g., each team member selects primary, elementary or middle school children); and d) compile responses/observations and discuss or write interpretations.

ACKNOWLEDGEMENTS

The authors would like to acknowledge the assistance of several individuals with reading, reviewing, and providing comments on sections of this manuscript. Thank you to Brenda Lee Love and Lisa Mehlig of Northern Illinois University; Patricia A. Graczyk of University of Illinois Chicago; Cathy S. Johnson of Custer Park Elementary School , Custer Park, Illinois; and Christen Brickert-Fuqua, Susan D. Hager, and Sharon L. Wolfe of DeKalb County Special Education Association, DeKalb, Illinois. Your assistance in the completion of this manuscript was very helpful and deeply appreciated. We would also like to thank our editor, Cara Harvey for all of her assistance.

We extend a special thanks to the child development instructors who provided us with feedback during the development of this guide:

Rosenna Bakari, State University of New York, Oneonta

Linda Bakken, Wichita State University

Reagan Curtis, Northwestern State University

William R. Fisk, Clemson University

Sue Grossman, Eastern Michigan University

Anne C. Lindsay, University of Arkansas, Little Rock

David Majsterek, Central Washington University

John R. McClure, Northern Arizona University

Kathy Morrison, University of Texas, Arlington

Brian Keith Salyer, Central Washington University

Vladimir M. Sloutsky, Ohio State University

Joan E. Test, Southern Illinois University

Ray Zarvell, Bradley University

A FINAL WORD

Our professional experiences working with children, college students, and educators have led us to plan this guide. It is our hope that through engaging in interviews and observations, educators will become hooked on using these techniques as tools for getting to know children better. As educators use these tools they are encouraged to reflect on the value of child development research for improving adult-child interactions and educational practices.

Denise H. Daniels
Lorrie J. Beaumont
Carol A. Doolin

An Introduction to Understanding Children

Understanding Children: An Interview and Observation Guide for Educators is a guide written for educators to gain a deeper insight into the physical, intellectual, and socioemotional development of children in primary through middle school. Children have different ways of thinking and perceiving the world,

CONTENTS

Why Is This Guide Important?

Sensitivity to Children

References

and adults find it difficult or impossible to return to childhood and try to view the world through their perspective. However, through carefully guided interviews and observation, educators *can* achieve a better understanding of children and their motives, thoughts, and behavior. Educational and developmental psychologists suggest that such insight is critical for providing supportive learning environments for all students (e.g., American Psychological Association Task Force 1993, 1997; National Association for the Education of Young Children, 1996; National Middle School Association, 1995).

Many factors influence how children are able to learn at school. For example, many children come to school feeling uneasy and vulnerable due to recurrent major adjustments they must make to new family structures, schools, and peer groups (Bronfenbrenner, 1986; Elkind, 1981). At the same time, they must adjust to rapid societal transitions brought about by technology. Many children handle these challenges with savvy and competence. Others need a great deal of support from teachers and other school personnel to adjust and learn. Developmental and educational theorists propose studying the child not in isolation but within his or her context (e.g., Bronfenbrenner, 1979; Bronfenbrenner & Morris, 1998, Vygotsky, 1978). This guide emphasizes looking at children in the context of schooling, in particular in connection with their teachers, classmates, and classroom environment.

The importance of the child-teacher relationship and interaction cannot be understated, especially for the child who is unable to find support and caring outside of school. Studies of resiliency in children point to the importance of a child establishing a relationship with a supportive, caring adult (Garmezy, 1985, 1993). Comer (1980) states, "the teacher is in a unique position somewhere between a parent and an evaluator. The sympathetic, trusted teacher who is less emotionally involved can help children understand that their feelings of worth and value grow from inner strength and can help the child see their positive qualities." Comer adds that "[positive] relationships with even withdrawn or antagonistic children can be established by listening, giving, being supportive" (pp. 170–171). Recent research suggests that perceived teacher support is important for all children's learning and adjustment (e.g., McCombs & Whisler, 1997; Pianta, 1999). By working to build a positive, supportive, and caring relationship with each child in the class, the teacher will enhance children's positive feelings about school and learning.

Relationships and interactions between classmates are also an important part of the child's context to consider. Children who respond and talk more in the classroom learn more than children who do not engage in classroom interaction (e.g., Cohen & Lotan, 1995). Teacher behavior can affect children's feelings of connectedness to the teacher as well as to their classmates. For example, Debra Skinner and her colleagues (1998) noted that children who feel their teacher is interested in them are more likely to perceive their environment as supportive and caring and thus engage in the classroom interactions that lead to greater learning and achievement. Interactions between classmates are also important as current curriculum, based on Vygotsky's (1978) theoretical work, often calls for students to support each other's learning through collaborative projects or peer tutoring. Research on assistance within the zone of proximal development has demonstrated how "more experienced others" help to bring students to a higher level of understanding and learning (e.g., Damon, 1984; Rogoff, 1990, 1998; Tharp & Gallimore, 1988). Peer acceptance is also a key to school adjustment (e.g., Ladd, 1996).

Children's perceptions of their classroom environment influence their academic achievement, and in a broader sense their development of the attitudes and behaviors needed to be successful (e.g., McCombs & Whisler, 1997; Vasquez, 1988). A variety of contextual clues influence children's perceptions of their classroom environment and their place within it. For example, teachers' facial expressions and feedback influence the formation of children's beliefs about their performance and acceptance in the classroom. Children also pay attention to the way the teacher and classmates respond to their questions, answers, and requests for help. Educators need to recognize that children attend to these responses as well as facial expressions and other non-verbal behavior (see Chapter 5) to form impressions of self and others. Children also attend to other features of the classroom environment, such as opportunities for making choices and engaging in interesting and challenging tasks.

WHY IS THIS GUIDE IMPORTANT?

Teachers' understanding of child development and of individual children's experiences, motives, and competencies will influence the way in which they teach (Meece, 2002; Olson & Bruner, 1996; Sigel & Kelley, 1988; Stott & Bowman, 1996). Unfortunately, research suggests that many educators may hold unrealistic expectations for children's development and do not always consider developmental appropriateness when planning instructional activities in their classrooms (e.g., Bryant, Clifford, & Peisner, 1991). These unrealistic expectations and developmentally inappropriate learning activities can limit children's potential for becoming successful learners. Other research findings suggest teachers' expectations of minority children or children from low-income families can affect children's opportunities to learn and prosper in the classroom (Gomez & Tabachnick, 1992). Louis (1994) explains that, "compared with teachers of more affluent children, teachers who work with students from poorer families are more likely to believe that their students bring behaviors into the classroom that make teaching difficult, and to believe that they have little influence over their students' learning. In addition, teachers in schools with a higher proportion of minority children are more likely to feel that their efforts in teaching are not rewarded with student engagement in learning" (p. 2). Carefully observing children's behavior, listening to what children are saying, and reflecting on this information in connection with theory and research on child development will help educators to make better choices in selecting appropriate learning activities. It will also help educators to think about their own style of teaching and how it connects them to the children in their classroom.

Kagan (1992) suggests that pre-service teachers' beliefs about students remain unchanged by their teacher education programs and follow them right into the classroom. Thus, many may enter the classroom with a significant lack of understanding about children (e.g., Sigel, 1990). Kagan's research showed that student teachers were more effective in their student teaching experiences when they attempted to understand children as individuals. For example, effective student teachers tended to see themselves as closely connected to their students' problems, and described their students' behavior in terms of their own attempts to intervene or their own affective responses to the students.

Educators will benefit from extended opportunities to interact with and study children in systematic ways such as through mini "research" assignments like the strategies proposed in this guide. These observation and interview strategies will allow educators to step back and reflect on their personal beliefs about the individual learner and the development of children in general. For the educator, this kind of reflective activity is essential for growth (e.g., Richardson, 1996). The strategies provided in this text will provide both pre-service and in-service teachers extended opportunities to get to know children. Professional associations such as the National Association for the Education of Young Children (NAEYC), acknowledge the value of this endeavor and specify that it is the teacher's responsibility to base instructional practices on solid knowledge of child development and even more importantly on "a particular knowledge of each child" in their standards for preparing educators to work with children (NAEYC, 1997, I-1.2).

In sum, we believe that educators will gain valuable insights into children's interests, concerns, thinking, and learning processes through the use of interviews and observations, just as developmental and educational psychologists have done (e.g., Duckworth, 1996; Good & Brophy, 2000; Siegler & Jenkins, 1989). Such insights are necessary for improving teaching effectiveness.

SENSITIVITY TO CHILDREN

Developmental and educational psychologists observe and interview children to better understand their unique perspectives on the world. For example, Eleanor Duckworth (1987), a student of Piaget's, attempted to understand children's "wonderful ideas" by using a clinical interview style (see Chapter 2) whereby her questions served as prompts and cues to help children expand their thinking and better explain themselves. She describes how important it is for teachers to be able to interpret the meaning of what children say and do. According to Duckworth,

> A good listener, or a good understander of explanations is aware that her first interpretation of what is being said may not be the right one and she keeps making guesses about what other interpretations are possible. This ability is

singularly undeveloped in little children, but it should be highly developed in good teachers. (p. 22)

She eloquently summarizes the importance of teacher sensitivity in the following statement,

> For me, through my experience with Piaget of working closely with one child at a time and trying to figure out what was really in that child's mind I have gained a wonderful background for being sensitive to children in the classroom. I think that a certain amount of this kind of background would be similarly useful for teachers. (p. 4)

The sensitivity Duckworth refers to is similar to Vygotsky's (1978) and, later, Rogoff's (1990) conceptualization of intersubjectivity. Intersubjectivity is defined as the mutual understanding that is achieved between people when they are communicating; this understanding cannot be attributed to one person or the other. Each participant in the conversation has to make some modification in order to reach an understanding of the other's perspective. The same can be said of the teacher-child interaction. When teachers develop an understanding of children, they are better able to guide their learning and plan appropriate instructional activities. The goal of this guide is to help educators develop such sensitivities to children in school settings.

REFERENCES

American Psychological Association Task Force on Psychology in Education (1993, 1997). *Learner-centered psychological principles: Guideline for school redesign and reform.* Washington, DC: American Psychological Association and Mid-Continent Regional Educational Laboratory.

Bronfenbrenner, U. (1979). *The ecology of human development: Experiments by nature and design.* Cambridge, MA: Harvard University Press.

Bronfenbrenner, U. (1986). Ecology of the family as a context for human development: Research perspectives. *Developmental Psychology, 22*(6), 723–742.

Bronfenbrenner, U., and Morris, P. (1998). The ecology of developmental processes. In W. Damon (Series Ed.) and R. Lerner (Vol. Ed.), *Handbook of Child Psychology: Vol 2. Theoretical Models of Human Development* (pp. 993–1028). New York: Wiley.

Bryant, D., Clifford, R., and Peisner, E. (1991). Best practices for beginners: Developmental appropriateness in kindergarten. *American Educational Research Journal, 28,* 783–803.

Cohen, E.G., and Lotan, RA (1995). Producing equal status interaction in the heterogeneous classroom. *American Educational Research Journal, 32*(1), 99–121.

Comer, J. P. (1980). *School power: Implications of an intervention project.* New York: The Free Press.

Damon, W. (1984). Peer education: The untapped potential. *Journal of Applied Developmental Psychology,* Vol. 5, 331–343.

Duckworth, E. (1996). *The having of wonderful ideas & other essays on teaching and learning,* 2nd ed. New York: Teachers College Press.

Duckworth, E. (1987). *The having of wonderful ideas & other essays on teaching and learning,* New York: Teachers College Press.

Elkind, D. (1981). *The hurried child.* Reading, MA: Addison-Wesley.

Garmezy, N. (1985). Stress-resistant children: The search for protective factors. In J. E. Stevenson (Ed.), *Recent Research in Developmental Psychopathology: Journal of Child Psychology and Psychiatry Book Supplement,* 4, 213–233.

Garmezy, N. (1993). Children in poverty: Resilience despite risk. *Psychiatry, 56,* 127–136.

Gomez, M. L. and Tabachnick, B. R. (1992). Telling teaching stories. *Teaching Education,* 4(2), 129–138.

Good, T. L., and Brophy, J. E. (2000). *Looking in classrooms.* New York: Longman.

Kagan, D. M. (1992). Professional growth among preservice and beginning teachers. *Review of Educational Research,* 62(2), 129–169.

Ladd, G. (1996). Shifting ecologies during the 5 to 7 year period: Predicting children's adjustment during the transition to grade school. In A. Sameroff and M. Haith (Eds.), *The five to seven year shift: The age of reason and responsibility.* Chicago, IL: University of Chicago Press.

Louis, K. S. (1994). Teacher engagement and real reform in urban schools. In B. Williams (Ed.), *Closing the achievement gap: A vision to guide change in beliefs and practice* (pp. 81–102). Philadelphia and Oak Brook, IL: Research for Better Schools and North Central Regional Educational Laboratory.

McCombs, B., and Whisler, J. (1997). The learner-centered classroom and school: Strategies for increasing student motivation and achievement. San Francisco: Jossey-Bass.

Meece, J. L. (2002). Child and adolescent development for educators. New York: McGraw-Hill.

National Association for the Education of Young Children, (1996). Guidelines for the preparation of early childhood professionals. Washington, DC: Author.

National Association for the Education of Young Children (1997). Code of ethical conduct. www.naeyc.org/about/position/pseth98.htm.

National Middle School Association (NMSA). (1995). This we believe. Columbus, OH: Author.

Olson, D. R., and Bruner, J. S. (1996). Folk psychology and folk pedagogy. In D. R. Olson and N. Torrance (Eds.), *The handbook of education and human development.* Malden, MA: Blackwell Publishers.

Pianta, R. (1999). *Enhancing relationships between children and teachers.* Washington, DC: American Psychological Association.

Richardson, V. (1996). The role of attitudes and beliefs in learning to teach. In J. Sikula, T. Buttery, and E. Guyton (Eds.), *Handbook of research on teacher education,* 2nd ed. New York: Prentice Hall.

Rogoff, B. (1990). *Apprenticeship in thinking: Cognitive development in social context.* New York: Oxford University Press.

Rogoff, B. (1998). Cognition as a collaborative process. In W. Damon (Series Ed.) and D. Kuhn and R. Siegler (Vol. Ed.) *Handbook of Child Psychology: Vol. 2. Cognition, Perception, and Language* (pp. 679–744). New York: Wiley.

Siegler, R. S., and Jenkins, E. (1989). *How children discover new strategies.* Hillsdale, NJ: Erlbaum.

Sigel, I. E., and Kelley, T. D. (1988). A cognitive developmental approach to questioning. In J. T. Dillon (Ed.), *Questioning and discussion: A multidisciplinary study.* Norwood, NJ: Ablexs.

Sigel, I. E. (1990). What teachers need to know about human development. In D. D. Dill and Associates (Eds.), *What teachers need to know.* San Francisco: Jossey-Bass.

Skinner, D., Bryant, D., Coffman, J., and Campbell, F. (1998). Creating risk and promise: Children's and teachers' co-constructions in the cultural work of kindergarten. The Elementary School Journal, 98(4), 297–310.

Stott, F., and Bowman, B. (1996). Child development knowledge: A slippery base for practice. Early Childhood Research Quarterly, 11, 169–183.

Tharp, R. G., and Gallimore, R. (1988). Rousing minds to life. New York: Cambridge University Press.

Vasquez, J. (1988). *Contexts of learning for minority students.* The Educational Forum, 52(3), 243–256.

Vygotsky, L. S. (1978). *Mind in society.* Cambridge, MA: Harvard University Press.

Interviewer/Observer Roles, Ethical Responsibilities, and Techniques

CHAPTER PREVIEW

We begin this chapter with a discussion of the role of the interviewer/observer in the classroom and the responsibilities associated with that role. Within this discussion, the consideration of children's rights and the importance of obtaining informed consent are emphasized. We then present an overview of observation and interview techniques that can be particularly useful for understanding child development in classroom settings. Many of the strategies contained in Chapters 3–5 use the techniques described in this chapter. However, we also outline techniques that observers and interviewers can apply on their own as they become more experienced. For example, they may want to develop their own set of questions using the clinical interview style suggested by the work of Jean Piaget and others (Duckworth, 1996; Ginsburg, 1997; Piaget, 1979). We encourage child study students to review this chapter and content in their child development text for clarification of techniques or definition of terms when using strategies contained in this supplemental text.

Our goal in this chapter is to provide practical and user-friendly techniques that will help develop a better understanding of the behaviors and thoughts of children. It is not our intent to present a comprehensive discussion of techniques used in research. Resources are listed at the end of the chapter to provide additional background about observation and interview techniques.

ROLES OF THE OBSERVER/INTERVIEWER

The student is considered a novice observer/interviewer who uses the child study process to learn about child development in a general sense and to gain practice in observing and interviewing children. However, teachers may use the child study process to learn more about individual children in their classroom or to better understand the group as a whole.

Regardless of their roles and purposes, observers and interviewers have an obligation to protect children and respect school personnel. Observers and interviewers are usually visitors in the classroom. In their role as visitors, they can only observe or interview children at the discretion of the classroom teacher. The presence of a visitor can be disruptive to the educational process; thus, visitors should be as unobtrusive as possible and responsive to the teacher's and children's preferences. If asked to leave, they must comply without question and then later contact the teacher to determine if another time would be more appropriate.

Local, state, and national teacher associations, including the National Association for the Education of Young Children (NAEYC) and the National Education Association (NEA), have official position statements regarding the ethical conduct of all educators. These statements reflect commitments to core values of the teaching profession. You are encouraged to review statements on the ethical responsibilities of educators as well as ethical guidelines for conducting research with children (see *Resources*). Although this is not intended to be a research guide, you should familiarize yourself with responsibilities and guidelines for conducting studies with children (see Table 2.1 for a brief summary of the Society of Research in Child Development's guidelines).

Institutional review boards are responsible for reviewing all research conducted in university classrooms involving human subjects. Although the strategies contained in this text are not intended to be used for research, we strongly urge students using this text to check with their instructors about their particular university's policies for conducting interviews and observations of children for assignments.

ETHICAL RESPONSIBILITIES AND CHILDREN'S RIGHTS

The protection of children's rights in any type of child study is imperative. Although observation strategies do not generally involve direct interaction with children, a two-way interaction between participants is inherent in the interview process. Regardless of the procedure used to collect information, the child's protection is paramount. The child must not come to any harm (i.e., physical or emotional) through participation in the observation and interview process. Observers and interviewers must consider potential negative effects they may have on the children, teachers, and other individuals in a classroom so that they do not inadvertently embarrass or cause undo stress and anxiety.

Confidentiality is another important ethical issue to be considered. Information obtained from observations or interviews must be handled with concern for the dignity of the child and the child's right to privacy. Information is to be kept confidential. The casual sharing of information collected about a child or teacher should be avoided at all times. The names of individuals should not be recorded in notes unless there is

Table 2.1

Guidelines for Conducting Research with Children

Source: SRCD Committee on Ethical Conduct in Child Development Research (1990)

1. In most cases, researchers must have their study reviewed by a school or institutional review board. Researchers must reveal all relevant information about the study.

2. Researchers must not use any methods or procedures that would cause physical or psychological harm to the child. The benefits of the study must outweigh its possible risks.

3. If participants are under the age of 18, researchers must inform the parents, guardians, or others responsible for the child's care about the research procedures and obtain their written consent before beginning the study.

4. If the participant is old enough to understand the research procedures, they must be informed and asked for their verbal consent before participating in the study. Participants must be informed that they can withdraw from the study at any time.

5. Researchers must keep all information about the participants confidential. In all reports of the investigation and in casual conversations about the study, the identities of the participants cannot be revealed.

6. Researchers must inform parents, guardians, or other responsible adults if they obtain information that threatens the child's well-being. For example, if during the study, the researcher discovers that a child is seriously depressed, the researcher must contact a person who can help the child obtain psychological treatment.

7. Each participant has a right to the results of the study. Researchers are obligated to share their research findings with interested parties (e.g., participants, parents, guardians, school officials and staff). As stated previously, the identities of the participants must be protected in research summaries.

8. Each child participant has the right to the benefits of a treatment provided to other participants. For example, if the experimental treatment is shown to be beneficial, then participants in the control group who did not receive the treatment have a right to beneficial treatments at some later time.

a professional reason for doing so (e.g. the observer is the child's teacher). Use of initials or codenames is a good substitute. The information collected should only be reported in the context of the learning assignment and then without the use of individuals' names or other identifying information. Informal discussion about individuals observed or interviewed is inappropriate. The exception to this rule would be if information is obtained that would suggest a safety concern for the child. In this case the information must be shared with school professionals who are in a position to assist the child as well as the child development course instructor.

In addition to rights protecting children's confidentiality, student observers/interviewers must discuss with their instructor the need for informing children's parents of the purpose of classroom observations (see Appendix A for a sample parent information letter). Students may need to obtain permission from parents for their child to be interviewed (see Appendix B for a sample parent consent form). Although when conducting interviews as part of a course requirement it may not require obtaining written consent from parents, we would still recommend doing so. Observer/interviewers can check with the school to determine what policies exist regarding the need for parental consent. The school may have a standard waiver used for many activities involving children. Interviewers should always ask for verbal assent or agreement from children prior to their participation in an interview. Children have the right to refuse to participate at any time during the interview or observation process and their wishes must be respected. Consideration of children's rights in the child study process is essential for maintaining the integrity of the interview/observation process.

OBSERVATION OVERVIEW

Observation tells us about children's behavior—what are they doing. It does not, however, tell us about their attitudes, understandings, or why they are doing what they are doing. For this reason, using observation and interview strategies together wherever possible is most effective (see Strategies 5.5–5.7 for example). This next section begins with a discussion of observation techniques because whenever possible at least some amount of casual observation should precede interviews.

Timing and Setting

If we want to understand children's development in school settings then we should observe them in these settings. Bronfenbrenner (1986) noted that studies of children in real-life settings can yield real-life applications. For example, Thorne (1993) observed children's social behaviors in the school lunchroom and on the playground. By observing children in these environments she was able to describe the authentic interactions of boys and girls as they move through their school day. Observation that takes place in a natural environment is referred to as **naturalistic observation**. Observers should apply the guide's Strategies in and around the classroom and playground the places children "naturally" spend their school day.

Preparation

Events in a classroom can move very quickly, and novice observers may not be accustomed to this pace. They also may become overwhelmed or distracted by the physical complexity of the classroom and all that is occurring (Good & Brophy, 2000). Therefore, we recommend that observers first casually observe a classroom or playground prior to conducting any of the strategies. Casual observation is that kind of "checking it out" that one might do before determining the "who" and "what" of observation. This provides some background and context for what will be seen when systematic observation strategies suggested in this guide are used. For example, casual observation of children playing together on the playground helps one become familiar with their use of slang or their "rules." Getting a "lay of the land" before observing in a classroom can prevent potential misunderstandings of what is seen later on.

Once you have become acclimated to the culture of schoolchildren, you are ready to practice systematic observation. Systematic observation serves a specific purpose and is carefully planned. When you are ready to move into a systematic style of observation the following decisions will have to be made. The following questions are adapted from Sommer and Sommer (1986).

Where will the observation take place? For example, if it is in the classroom, where will you place yourself? In the back of the room? Sitting at a table with the children? Sitting in a child's desk? It is important that you are comfortable and look as natural as possible so that children and other school personnel are not distracted.

When will the observation be conducted? For example, will it be when school starts or right after lunch? Plan to arrive a few minutes before the children so you can already be in place when they enter the classroom. If arriving during the middle of the school day, be extra sensitive about interrupting what is taking place in the classroom.

Who will be the target of the observation? For example, is it one child or a small group of children?

What will the observer be looking for? For example, are you watching for a particular behavior? Observing children's responses to the teacher? Observing interactions among children? Observers must operationalize, or define, what they are observing; otherwise they may be distracted by other activities and lose their focus. Operationalizing the "what" involves observers defining or describing the behaviors they are interested in observing. Some sample operational definitions of behavior categories are provided in the Strategies.

Qualities of a Good Observer

There are a number of specific qualities of observers that make them effective when observing children in school settings. The following suggestions are adapted from Garbarino, Stott, and their colleagues' (1992) work. Good observers…

Recognize personal biases and preconceived assumptions about children. As an observer you need to be able to get out of the way of your thoughts and emotions to objectively focus on what you are seeing in children's behavior. One common bias concerns gender roles. For example, Vivian Paley (1984) was more tolerant of young boys' rambunctious behavior in her kindergarten class than of girls. She recognized this gender role expectation for boys to be louder and more active than girls as a personal bias and thus was eventually able to look past it and focus more objectively on the children's behavior.

Stay focused for a long period of time on whatever is being observed. Being in a comfortable position while observing can enhance your concentration. Thus you are better able to recognize extraneous stimuli (e.g., student movement, class transitions) and tune them out. The effective observer finds ways to prevent distractions and stay focused on the child or activities he or she is observing.

Pay attention to the details. Details include nonverbal cues in the environment, such as children's facial expressions and classroom atmosphere. Good observers write details and impressions in their field notes and decide later what should be included in analysis or reports.

Maintain flexibility.   Observers frequently need to alter locations and plans. For example, observers may find that they are physically in the way of the children or the teacher and therefore need to change locations more than once during the observation so they do not disrupt the flow of classroom activities. Observers may need to change locations and plans due to disruptions in children's activities. Observers also may need to adjust their plans when, for example, they find their coding schemes are not working as expected and they need to add or delete categories. In the meantime, they make the best use of their time and make formal revisions away from the classroom.

Use the least intrusive form for recording observations.   The best way to blend in is to use tools familiar to children in classrooms such as notepads or pencil. The use of video cameras and cassette recorders should be limited to special cases and only with clear permission from the child development instructor, classroom teacher, and parents.

OBSERVATION TECHNIQUES

Child study students should try the following systematic observation techniques commonly used in research with children. These techniques are appropriate for observing in classrooms and will reveal developmental differences and similarities among school-age children. All of these techniques require advance planning.

Event Sampling

Event sampling allows one to focus on a particular event of interest. For example, in Strategy 5.7, we suggest that you observe individual children as they initiate interactions with their teachers. In using Strategy 3.3, you will observe students' physical activities during the day, in particular, when children change activities or move about the classroom.

In using this technique, observations are triggered by specific events, thus allowing the observer to monitor several children at one time. One of the disadvantages of this method is that events are seen out of context. An advantage of this method is that it can help to document behaviors or events that occur infrequently. For example educators may want to document children's behavior in a school cafeteria because they have a hunch that bullying and intimidation are occurring at this time (Isaksen, 1986). In this instance in using the event sampling technique, the observer focuses only on those behaviors that are occasions of bullying or intimidation.

Time Sampling

Time sampling can reveal consistent patterns in children's behavior that occur over a span of time. With this technique, observers record particular behaviors for a short period of time, often 10–15 minutes. Behaviors are usually recorded in the form of tallies on a predetermined coding sheet, or **checklist**, and then subjected to a frequency count. This makes recording behaviors quick and efficient because the observer does not need to do a lot of writing as in other techniques.

Strategies 5.10 and 5.13 are examples of observation strategies using the time sampling technique. In Strategy 5.10 you will watch five children for one minute each, noting their play behavior and social interactions. Categories of behavior are provided and you check the behaviors and interactions that you see each minute. Strategy 5.13 asks you to focus on a child for 10 minutes and note specific attending behaviors such as being on or off task.

Time samples can be conducted at different times during the same day, or the same time on different days depending on the purpose of the observation. One disadvantage of this method is that it requires a strong focus and deep level of concentration. Observers cannot expect to conduct very many time samples in a given day. They should take breaks between each observation. Like event sampling, this technique also focuses on behavior and ignores the context. Disregarding the context may lead to biased or inaccurate interpretation (Beaty, 1994). The main advantage of time sampling is that it allows for carefully controlled observations and can yield fairly objective results.

Anecdotal Records

Anecdotal records are short, narrative descriptions that are written down immediately after the behavior or event occurs. Educators can use these to take a quick snapshot of a child's behavior. They jot down quick descriptions and later record some of their inferences or impressions about it. This method is effective in capturing whatever seems important at a given time. For instance, if a classroom teacher is concerned about a child's shyness and lack of social adjustment to the classroom, he or she will want to note the occasions when he or she sees the child approach another child to initiate play. Strategy 4.9 employs this technique to capture school children's use of satire and metaphor in conversation.

The advantage of anecdotal records is that they are open-ended and can provide rich details about a child or event (e.g., Beaty, 1994). Their limitation is that events must be described soon after they happen or the observer may forget important information. Anecdotal records can provide rich information for sharing with parents at conferences. For efficient recording of anecdotes, observers will need to have a notebook, index cards, or other workable tool on hand so that they are always prepared to record.

Running Record

A running record is a thorough narrative description of a child's behavior as it occurs sequentially. The purpose of a running record is to capture as many details as possible so that another observer could read the notes and get an accurate and vivid picture of the behavior or event. Observers record as many details of an event or behavior as possible to construct a complete record of the occurrence. They decide as they go along what behaviors are irrelevant or perhaps insignificant. This can leave *important* holes or missing details in the description. The running record is not the first choice of many child observers because of the time it takes to record and then to analyze. It also takes quite a bit of practice to become skilled at this technique. A running record is usually used to observe only one child at a time. It can be used to record interactions between two children, but the risk of missing details then increases.

In Strategy 4.1, you will observe two children engaged in play. You are asked to record all of the behaviors and exact words of children for approximately 15 minutes. In analyzing your notes you will look for evidence of children's cognitive processes and competencies, such as perspective taking and the understanding of game rules. This running record has a time limit and asks you to only look at two children, so it should not be too difficult or overwhelming if you use abbreviations in your note taking.

Checklists and Rating Scales

Two primary tools are recommended for recording observational data: checklists and rating scales. These tools are used in many of the text's strategies (e.g. Strategies 3.1, 3.5, 3.6, 3.7, 5.3, 5.11, and 5.14) because of their ease of use and the amount of information they can provide. Checklists are a listing of behaviors or characteristics of an interaction where one records the behaviors' presence or absence by using tallies or check marks. These are generally easy to use as long as the categories listed are clear and describe observable behaviors. Checklists must be prepared in advance of an observation session. Observers need to be very clear about what it is they want to look at or look for. The behaviors or characteristics should be logically organized and should appropriately serve the purposes of the observation.

Checklists can be used quickly and efficiently, and can be used to look at more than one child at a time. They are especially useful for looking at an entire class. Checklists can be adapted as they are used. For instance if particular behaviors are never observed, they can be removed from the checklist. Similarly if new relevant behaviors are seen frequently then they should be added to the checklist. The main disadvantage of a checklist is that it provides little description about the context in which the behavior occurs. It may answer the "what" questions but does not answer the "how" or "why" questions (Beaty, 1994).

A rating scale is a quantitative judgment that uses numbers to rate the occurrence or strength of a particular characteristic one has observed. For example, Strategy 3.7 asks you to rate the complexity of playground equipment. Rating scales also can be used to judge the degree to which a child exhibits a particular behavior (e.g., pro-social, aggression). This tool is constructed before the observation session. If well constructed, it is easy to use and takes little time to complete. It is also useful for observing more than one child or feature of the environment at a time. The main disadvantage of using a rating scale is that it is a subjective tool. When two or more observers are using the same rating scale to conduct similar observations, they can compare their results to determine observer agreement or interrater reliability. Reliable checklists result in high observer agreement. We will return to this topic when we discuss interpretation of observations.

Summary of Observation Techniques

The observation techniques we have described are relatively simple to learn, and become easier to use with practice. Many of the observation strategies contained in this text incorporate these techniques (see Table 2.2). As we have suggested, before starting any kind of systematic observation, child study students should try to spend some time casually observing the classroom or school playground. They will need to carefully review the strategies and perhaps refer to this chapter to review the techniques and tips on being an effective observer. We hope that educators will construct their own unique observation sessions to investigate specific behaviors or activities occurring in their classrooms. Additional background on conducting observations with children can be found in the resources listed at the end of this chapter.

Strategy	Observation/Interview Technique
3.1: Observations of Body Growth and Physical Development	Checklist
3.2: Perceptions of Attractiveness Interview	Semi-structured Interview
3.3: Observation of School Day Activity	Event Sampling
3.4: Preferred Physical Activities Interview	Semi–structured Interview
3.5: Observation of Children's Handwriting Skills and Drawing	Checklist
3.6: Observations of Gross Motor Skills in School Settings	Checklist
3.7: Playground Environment Checklist/Rating Scale	Checklist/Rating Scale
3.8: Observations of Playground Behavior	Checklist
3.9: Visit with the School Nurse	Structured Interview
4.1: Observation of Cognitive Processes Revealed in Play	Running Record
4.2: Guided Participation: Play with Peers and Adults	Running Record
4.3: Perspective Tasks and Dilemmas	Combination
4.4: Conservation Tasks	Semi-structured Interview
4.5: Classes and Relations	Combination
4.6: Hypotheses Testing	Combination
4.7: Arithmetic Strategies	Combination
4.8: Reading Strategies and Purposes	Semi-structured Interview/Combine
4.9: Use of Language: Conversation, Metaphor, and Satire	Anecdotal Record/Combination
4.10: Memory Awareness and Self-Monitoring	Structured Interview
4.11: Planning and Problem-solving	Combination
4.12: Instructional Interactions with Teachers and Peers	Combination
4.13: Interview with a Teacher	Semi-structured Interview
5.1: Identifying Facial Expressions	Structured Interview/Rating
5.2: Self-Description	Semi-structured Interview
5.3: Perceptions of Competence	Rating Scale, Semi-structured Int.
5.4: Hypothetical Classmates' Behavior	Rating Scale
5.5: What is a Good Teacher?	Semi-structured Interview
5.6: Quality of Relationship with Teacher	Rating Scale/Semi-structured Int.
5.7: Observations of Student–Teacher Interactions	Event Sampling
5.8: What is a Friend?	Semi-structured Interview
5.9: Quality of Peer Relationships	Semi-structured Interview
5.10: Observations of Social Interactions & Play	Time Sampling
5.11: Perceptions of Social Support	Structured Interview/Rating Scale
5.12: Views of Schoolwork	Semi-structured Interview
5.13: Observation of Student Engagement	Time Sampling
5.14: Classroom Environment Survey	Rating Scale

Table 2.2
Observation/Interview Techniques Used in the Strategies

INTERVIEW OVERVIEW

Ideally, observations should be supported by interviews. In several of the strategies offered in Chapters 3–5, we suggest using observation and interviews together. Using both methods can help educators arrive at a more comprehensive understanding of children and classroom activities. For example, Siegler (1996) combined observation and interview to understand children's strategies for solving arithmetic problems. Observations of behavior alone do not promote a full understanding of children's perspectives. Observations used alone present two major challenges (Piaget, 1979). First, observations do not capture children's thinking. Children require the assistance of a good questioner to help them elaborate their ideas. Children may hold back what they know because they assume the adults around them already know it. Or they may be concerned that if they do try to explain their thinking, they will be wrong. Without the careful questioning of an experienced adult, many of children's inexpressible thoughts will remain unknown. Second, when observing children it is difficult to ascertain whether their behavior reflects their actual thoughts and feelings. Interviews can reveal such discrepancies. For example, children may appear motivated to perform a task through their behavior, but interviews may reveal their lack of interest or understanding.

Children understand their own child culture and are generally happy to tell us about it if we are willing to listen and learn from them. Educators must enter interview situations with the basic assumption that while adults may have difficulty with understanding children's responses, those responses make sense to the child.

Timing and Setting

In a good interview, timing can be everything (Graue & Walsh, 1998). Trying to talk to a child when he or she is in the middle of an interesting activity is futile. Likewise, talking to a child at the end of a tiring day also can be unproductive. Another bad time for conducting an interview is when the child is actively engaged with friends. It is best if interviewers use some of the "down time" during the day to conduct interviews. This may be during quiet reading or when students are working on seatwork. The goal is to find a time when sitting and talking to an adult is appealing to children.

The setting or location where the interview takes place is important as well. Some interviews can be conducted in the classroom, but many times it is easier to use a hallway, conference room, or even the school's learning center. These areas can provide quiet and less distraction for the child than the classroom allows. The child study student may need to make arrangements in advance with the classroom teacher for an area conducive for interviewing.

Preparation

Child study students can use some of the same suggestions in preparing to interview as they do in preparing to observe. That is, spending time in advance casually observing children in classrooms or on the school playground can familiarize the interviewer with children's language, slang, and general behaviors. This will become important when the interviewer tries to establish rapport with the child—a very important first step in the interview process.

In addition it would be beneficial for child study students to consult their child development text and review, for example, Piaget's stages of cognitive development (e.g., preoperational, concrete operational, formal operational), as well as research on language development. This review will help in the interpretation and analysis of the child's words.

It is essential when planning an interview with children that the most appropriate questioning techniques are selected. Two types of questions that work well when interviewing children are hypothetical and third-person questions (Graue & Walsh, 1998). Both of these types of questions keep children from feeling "on the spot" during the interview (see strategy 5.4 for an example). Hypothetical questions can turn the interview into a kind of pretend play for the child, and this can be particularly helpful when working with younger children. Older children are not as intimidated by interview questions and may not feel as pressured to give the "right" answer. Hypothetical questions might begin with phrases such as "Suppose you were," "What if you," or "Pretend that." These kinds of questions allow the child a degree of emotional distance by adding a gamelike quality to the interview. Third-person questions can be about kids in general rather than targeting the child being interviewed, for instance: "What do you think most boys like to do during recess?" or "What kind of subjects do girls like in school?" Again, general questions are less intimidating and do not invade the child's privacy. This kind of questioning can put children in roles as "experts," which makes them feel good about themselves.

Qualities of a Good Interviewer

There are a number of qualities of a good interviewer. Holmes (1998) and others propose that good interviewers...

Consider the relationship between the child and the interviewer.   The child's perception of the interviewer can affect the success of the conversation or interview. It is important to consider if children feel comfortable and safe, or anxious with the interviewer.

Consider factors such as race, ethnicity, gender, or physical characteristics that can have an impact on the child.   Research indicates that children are not as affected by an interviewer's ethnicity as they are by gender (Holmes, 1998). Children tend to be more tolerant and accepting than adults, perhaps because of their increased experiences with individuals from diverse backgrounds.

Gender factors appear to influence children in interview situations. Researchers who have studied children have determined that female interviewers tend to be seen as more accessible and less threatening than male interviewers (Holmes, 1998). Female interviewers have a size advantage over males. They are closer in size to the children and, thus, have an easier time fitting in child-sized furniture and looking children in the eye. Men with facial hair also may be intimidating to children, especially the younger ones. Another possible reason that children see male interviewers as intimidating is that their experience with males in school is often in their roles as principals. Children may perceive males as having more authority in the school setting, and therefore feel less at ease when talking with them.

Consider how interviewer bias and/or gender may affect interpretations.   Adults may make assumptions about children from particular ethnic groups that are projected on the child they are interviewing. The gender of the interviewer can influence interpretations of the child's words. Interviewers may be confused by a child's report of an experience because they did not experience it themselves as a little boy or girl. For instance, a male interviewer may have difficulty relating to a girl discussing her Barbie collection. A female interviewer may not respond well to discussion about wrestling. Interviewers need to recognize these biases and account for them as they try to make sense of what the child is saying.

Consider voice tone and the use of age-appropriate vocabulary.   Children in a classroom are accustomed to being asked questions by the teacher regarding academic subjects or their behavior in an authoritative "teacher voice." For conducting the kind of interviews we are advocating in this text, interviewers need to change the tone of their voices during questioning in order to put children at ease. To some extent, it is appropriate for interviewers to assume a kind of "kid-talk" rather than "teacher-talk" when interviewing children. This is another reason we suggest spending plenty of time "hanging out" around children to learn to model this type of speech. This hanging out time is actually a disciplined and systematic way to understand children who are smarter than we are about their world.

Consider potential "adult" biases.   Good interviewers need to be able to "get out of their own way" so to speak, so that they do not find themselves over- or underanalyzing what they are seeing and hearing. Adults can limit their understandings by a tendency to process the child's words through their own view of the world. The child's view may be qualitatively different.

Ask good questions.   Sometimes the problem in an unsuccessful interview is that the child cannot understand what the adult is asking. Jean Piaget (1979) proposed a developmental hierarchy of comprehending responses that children exhibit when being interviewed. Piaget begins at the lowest level of a child's understanding when the child has not understood the question or simply doesn't care about it. This child will give a random answer that is no help to the interviewer. In this case it may be that the interviewer has to simplify her language to make questions more clear and concise. As the interviewer's questions become clearer to the child, he or she will draw on previous experience or knowledge to formulate an answer. In some cases, if the child is just not interested in the interview, a short answer will be given that the child thinks sounds good and will satisfy the adult who is asking the questions. However, in these cases, the interviewer cannot assume that the answer reveals the true measure of the child's understanding. In Piaget's discussions of clinical interviews, he suggests that effective interviewers may have to reformulate their questions multiple times in order to get at the deepest level of a child's thought.

Are good listeners.   The ability to really listen is a key factor in any interview. Interviewers need to focus all of their attention on the child. They must not only be attentive to what is being said but also to how it is being said. Sometimes interviewers will have to depend on other signals, such as the child's eyes or body language, to gauge the effectiveness of the interview.

Are well versed in child development theory and research.   Interviewers with greater knowledge of child development will be better prepared to identify effective questions for children and interpret their responses. For example, well-informed interviewers can anticipate that younger children are more apt to provide an answer, whether right or wrong, simply because they are seeking approval. They also may acknowledge that older children's social concerns (e.g., "What will the other kids think of me?") may lead to difficulties with communicating.

INTERVIEW TECHNIQUES

An Introduction to Structured and Semi-Structured Interviews

There are several interview techniques that are particularly effective for enhancing understanding of the cognitive processes and feelings of children. We will refer to two categories of interviews: structured or semi-structured. Structured interviews typically have predetermined questions that are the means to an end, such as asking, "What is your favorite subject in school?" to find out, for instance, if more boys than girls report liking mathematics. Some structured interviews are conducted using a questionnaire so that the interviewer sticks to specific questions. These interviewers are concerned about getting offtrack when the child goes off on a tangent.

Structured interviews can work well in particular cases, such as when an educator wants to talk with several students about a very specific subject and has limited time. A benefit of structured interviews is that they are relatively easy to conduct. The questions are posed just as they are worded in the prepared list or questionnaire, and then the children's answers are written down exactly as they state them. Another benefit of structured interviews is that all children will be asked the same questions in the same way. In this way, interviewers can better control the interview process. These questions can be kept brief so that the interviewer does not worry about losing a child's attention and also has time to talk to more children.

One of the challenges of structured interviewing is that if the child does not understand a question, the interviewer is not free to clarify or expand on it so that the child can give a more informed answer (Piaget, 1979). As a result, structured interviews can be perceived by children as a test and therefore produce anxiety. Children answering structured interview questions may give short answers and seek approval from the interviewer (especially younger children). They may feel the goal of the interviewer is to find out if they know the right answer. Another limitation with using structured interviews is that they do not allow full exploration of the child's thinking or reasoning. Interviewers might be able to find out what the child knows or does not know but will not be able to find out the extent of the child's understanding. Furthermore, these interviews cannot determine how children arrived at their understandings or misunderstandings. In a structured interview, novice interviewers may miss what children are telling them "between the lines."

Often in the classroom, teachers do not have time to conduct preplanned, structured interviews. However, they should always be prepared to talk to a child spontaneously. These short conversations with individual children over the course of a day or week can add up to rich and useful anecdotal information. Teachers must be prepared at short notice to initiate or continue a conversation with a student. This concept is similar to the idea of the "teachable moment." This idea suggests that a good teacher is always prepared to use spontaneous ideas or experiences in the classroom as opportunities to teach potentially valuable lessons to their students.

A semi-structured interview incorporates more open-ended questions and may not have a specific goal. These kinds of interviews work especially well with younger children who may have difficulties with language competence and understanding questions. Interviewers use just a few general questions but allow the child to do all of the explaining of their answers. The advantage of the semi-structured interview is that it provides a framework of questions to focus the interviewer while at the same time allowing for the child's thoughts to emerge through his or her answers.

The major limitation of semi-structured interviewing is time. There is no way to plan in advance how long an interview like this will take. It might take a while to get the child started. Interviewers using this method need to be skilled at asking effective probing or follow-up questions. The child might take the interviewer off into a whole new direction that, while not planned, becomes very interesting. The interaction between interviewer and child is key to a successful semi-structured interview. The process cannot be rushed, and interviewers have to be comfortable with occasional periods of silence from the child. However, if a semi-structured interview is not going well, not moving along in any particular direction, the child or interviewer may decide to end it abruptly. This type of interviewing is one that requires a rather extensive understanding of child development to help determine how best to phrase the questions, how to interpret the child's body language, and how to interpret the interview

In this text, there are several semi-structured interviews. These interviews include some predetermined questions; however, they tend to be rather open-ended in their tone (see Strategies 3.2, 3.4, 4.6, 5.5, and 5.12). There is still opportunity in these types of interviews for children to elaborate on their answers. The interviewer is looking for the child's perspective rather than for the right answer. In many of the interview strategies, probes to help children expand on their answers and elaborate on their perspective are suggested.

Clinical Interview Method

A classic example of the semi-structured interview comes from the work of Piaget (1979). In his work with children, he often used a form of interview that he adapted from his work in clinical psychology. He found this clinical style of interviewing was quite suitable for understanding children's thinking, which he believed was qualitatively different than that of adults. (Refer to your child development text for a thorough discussion of Piaget's theory of cognitive development). According to Piaget, the clinical interview style is a flexible method that allows the child's answers to provide direction to the questioning. If the child says something interesting interviewers can immediately pursue it and get the child to expand on his or her reasoning. The clinical method follows the child's own line of thought without imposing a particular direction. Its aim is to truly understand the reasoning behind the child's answers. In his writings, Piaget (1979) has given us clear guidelines for conducting clinical interviews with children.

1. Try to adopt the language of the child and keep the level of questioning accessible to the child. Use simple words and short sentences as is appropriate for the age of the child

2. Begin with an open-ended question such as, "Tell me about your school." Piaget suggests that interviewers come up with their questions by listening to the spontaneous questions of children the same age or younger. As we have suggested, child study students should casually observe children in the classroom to "listen in" on their conversations and questions.

3. If necessary, rephrase the question, and then do it again, and again, until the child gives some kind of response (see *Qualities of a Good Interviewer* earlier in this chapter). Improvisation is a constant necessity in conducting clinical interviews with children. Knowing how to conduct a good interview with children is truly an art.

4. As the child responds to the question, the interviewer should begin to form a hypothesis about the child. For instance, if a child is talking about school, the interviewer may determine that this child does not enjoy school for some reason.

5. Use follow-up questions to explore your hypothesis. Continuing with our example above, "What are some things you don't really like about school?"

6. Challenge the child's responses and see if the child will defend or reject them. For example, "School is no fun, right?" or "I never liked school when I was growing up."

7. Allow the child's answers to lead you to a correct interpretation.

8. Be careful not to overreact to their responses, either positively or negatively—for example, "You're kidding!" or "Wow, that's the most amazing thing I've ever heard!"

The second author has conducted many clinical interviews with children participating in museum programs. During one interview, she asked a small group of fourth grade students how they came to be involved in a particular museum program about rivers and conservation. As the students began to describe the selection process, she noticed one boy was not contributing anything to the conversation. She asked him how he became involved, and he responded that "basically I am a bad kid" but that this time his teacher had decided to give him a chance "and now I'm a leader in deforestation!" She then turned the conversation to talking about how this program was different from regular schoolwork, hypothesizing that this was the reason a child like him might be able to be successful. She continued talking to him for a few minutes so that he could explain to her why he felt that it was important that he was "a leader in deforestation." The boy's contribution to the interview changed the direction of the questioning, not only in this case, but with future groups of children and teachers. The interviewer wanted to see if what the boy told her was true for other students as well. The clinical interview method allowed the interviewer to follow the boy's line of thinking until she came to the conclusion *he* was trying to make.

Piaget's clinical method of interviewing has been compared to Socratic questioning used by teachers throughout the history of education. Ginsburg (Ginsburg, Jacobs, & Lopez 1997; 1998) believes that the clinical method is very appropriate for examining a child's understanding of academic subject matter. He further notes that the clinical method is particularly valuable in identifying intellectual difficulties that may be responsible for learning problems. Duckworth (1996) and Gallas (1995) also have used the clinical interview method to explore children's theories and ideas.

Adaptations of the Clinical Interview Method

Other researchers in child development have used variations of the clinical interview method to understand children's theories and cognitive processes. Siegler (1996) suggested the microgenetic method as an effective means for learning about children's strategies for problem solving in areas such as mathematics. The microgenetic method combines short observational periods and clinical style interviewing while children are solving problems. The goal of this method is to examine children's thinking in process.

Vosniadou (1994) used generative interviews to understand children's mental models of the earth. Like clinical interviews, generative interviews follow the child's thought processes. The generative interview differs from Piaget's clinical interview in that children's beliefs are not challenged or contradicted in any way by the interviewer (see the steps for conducting a clinical interview). Follow-up questions are asked as a way of probing deeper into the child's understanding.

Summary of Interview Techniques

The kinds of interviewing techniques that we have described give the child study student an opportunity to understand the child's perspective. If adults can get out of their own way and really listen to what children are telling them, they will have a much better sense of what children believe and understand about their world. Some of the strategies in this text incorporate suggestions for conducting semi-structured interviews (see Table 2.2), providing a framework of questions while still allowing interviewers to probe children's thinking further. Child study students also may find the other kinds of techniques introduced here helpful in finding ways to better understand children's perspectives.

INTERPRETING AND UNDERSTANDING OBSERVATIONS AND INTERVIEWS

The interpretation or analysis of observations should begin while the observer is in the "field" or classroom. Some observers write memos to themselves while conducting the observation (Maxwell, 1996). These are notes indicating inferences the observer is beginning to make, issues of bias they may be noting in themselves, and questions about the observation they want to answer or reflect on more at a later time. If observers make these kinds of written "mental notes" as they are conducting an observation, it will help in the interpretation phase later on.

If observers use narrative techniques such as running anecdotal records, the first step is to thoroughly read through their rough notes. Some observers at this stage make written notes to themselves in the margins where they describe patterns that are emerging in the behavior they observed.

As observers begin to notice patterns of behavior, they can assign category names or codes to these behaviors. A classic study done by Mildred Parten (1932) involved observing children engaged in free play in nursery schools. In analyzing these data, Parten derived six categories of play to which she assigned the codes unoccupied play, solitary play, onlooker play, parallel play, associative play, and cooperative play. Later, researchers assigned new categories to children's play, such as sensorimotor/practice play, pretend/symbolic play, constructive play, and games.

Codes and categories are subjective. They are the lens through which the observer is choosing to view the "world" (Sommer & Sommer, 1986). The codes must fit the purposes of the observation very clearly. Terms and operational definitions must be clear. In many cases more than one observer will use the observation tool, so it is imperative that these terms be defined clearly. For instance, if a code in a particular observation is *interaction*, observers need to define whether the interaction is child/child, teacher/child, teacher/teacher, and so on. Several strategies in this guide have codes or categories already determined. Codes and categories may have to be modified as observers work with them. For example, a new behavior may emerge that does not fit a code. The observer considers the context of this new behavior and decides whether or not to modify an existing code or develop a new one.

If two or more individuals are conducting an observation using the same coding scheme, they can compare findings to see if there is agreement. This is referred to as interobserver or intercoder reliability. If there is disagreement, observers may need to look carefully at the description of the code or rating, or the particular directions for the observation task, to be sure there isn't a simple misunderstanding. A simple formula for computing a percentage agreement score is

Total number of agreements

divided by

Total number of observations (# of agreements + # of disagreements)

Observers and interviewers follow similar procedures in analyzing responses or behavior. After transcribing interviews, interviewers look carefully through transcripts for patterns or categories of responses.

Suggestions for interpreting observation and interview data are provided after each strategy in Chapters 3–5. The interpretations tie observations and interviews to child development theories and research. Chapter 6 demonstrates how data can be integrated in the writing of two child profiles. We expect that as observers/interviewers become more experienced using the sample strategies provided, they will want to design some of their own. At that point, it would be helpful to return to this chapter (including the *Resources*) and their child development text to review techniques for conducting and interpreting observations and interviews. Our goal is to encourage child study students and educators to use observation and interviews with children as a way of entering their worlds and thereby coming to a better understanding of their development.

RESOURCES

Good, T. L., and Brophy, J. E. (2000). *Looking into classrooms.* New York: Longman.

Graue, M. E., and Walsh, D. J. (1998). *Studying children in context.* Thousand Oaks, CA: Sage Publications.

Greig, A., and Taylor, J. (1999). *Doing research with children.* Thousand Oaks, CA: Sage Publications.

Holmes, R. M. (1998). *Fieldwork with children.* Thousand Oaks, CA: Sage Publications.

Isaksen, J. G. (1986). *Watching and wondering.* Palo Alto, CA: Mayfield Publishing Company.

National Association for the Education of Young Children (1997). *Code of ethical conduct.* www.naeyc.org/about/position/pseth98.htm.

Society for Research in Child Development. www.srcd.org/about.html#standards.

Sommer, R., and Sommer, B. B. (1986). *A practical guide to behavioral research: Tools and techniques.* New York: Oxford University Press.

REFERENCES

Beaty, J. J. (1994). *Observing development of the young child.* New York: Macmillan Publishing Company.

Bronfenbrenner, U. (1986). Ecology of the family as a context for human development.: Research perspectives. *Developmental Psychology, 22* (6), 723–742.

Duckworth, E. (1996). *The having of wonderful ideas & other essays on teaching and learning.* New York: Teacher's College Press.

Gallas, K. (1995). *Talking their way into science: hearing children's questions and theories, responding with curricula.* New York: Teacher's College Press.

Garbarino, J., Stott, F. M., and the Faculty of the Erikson Institute (1992). *What children can tell us: Eliciting, interpreting, and evaluating critical information from children.* San Francisco: Jossey-Bass.

Ginsburg, H., and Opper, S. (1979). *Piaget's Theory of Intellectual Development.* NJ: Prentice Hall.

Ginsburg, H. (1997). *Entering the child's mind: The clinical interview in psychological research and practice.* New York: Cambridge University Press.

Ginsburg, H. P., Jacobs, S. F., and Lopez, L. S. (1998). *Teacher's guide to flexible interviewing in the classroom: Learning what children know about math.* Boston: Allyn and Bacon.

Maxwell, J. A. (1996). *Qualitative research design: An interactive approach.* Thousand Oaks, CA: Sage Publications.

Paley, V. G. (1984). *Boys and girls: Superheroes in the doll corner.* Chicago, IL: The University of Chicago Press.

Parten, M. (1932). Social participation among preschool children. *Journal of Abnormal and Social Psychology, 27,* 243–269.

Piaget, J. (1979). *The child's conception of the world.* Totowa, NJ: Littlefield, Adams and Co.

Siegler, R. S. (1996). *Emerging minds: The process of change in children's thinking.* New York: Oxford University Press..

Thorne, B. (1993). *Gender play: Girls and boys in school.* New Brunswick, NJ: Rutgers University Press.

Vosniadou, S. (1994). Universal and culture-specific properties of children's mental models of the earth. In L. A. Hirschfeld and S. A. Gelman (Eds.), *Mapping the mind: Domain specificity in cognition and culture* (pp. 412–430). New York: Cambridge University Press.

Vosniadou, S., and Brewer, W. F. (1992). Mental models of the earth: A study of conceptual change in childhood. *Cognitive Psychology, 24,* 535–585.

Physical Development

CHAPTER PREVIEW

Chapter 3 begins with a look at children's physical growth and perceptions of body shape, followed by an investigation of physical activity and motor skills. Children's socialization and play behaviors on the playground are studied in addition to the playground itself as a setting for motor skill development and practice. The chapter concludes with a general look at children's health as seen through the eyes of the school nurse. Observation and interview strategies provide insight into how children's physical growth and development can influence children's general school performance.

BODY GROWTH AND DEVELOPMENT

Body growth is an important aspect of physical development. Changes in children's height, weight, and body shape during the elementary school years are easily observed and frequently noticed by teachers. Educators' personal attitudes toward body shape can affect the way they teach (Bennett, 1991). Therefore an investigation of body size and shape is important to enhance educators' understanding of children's growth and development and how individual differences can influence their perceptions of children and instructional interactions.

Body image and self image are closely related for the elementary-age child. Children's perceptions of their physical appearance have been found to be important in how they develop self-esteem, construct interpersonal relationships with classmates and adults, and

CONTENTS

define themselves (Harter, 1990, Hughes, Noppe, & Noppe, 1996). A better understanding of how children perceive themselves and their bodies can help teachers enhance their success in school.

Height, Weight, and Body Shape

The following observation strategy (Strategy 3.1) seeks to make salient the differences in children's growth rates during the elementary and middle school years. This strategy requires the observer to observe height, weight, and body shapes in an investigation of the size differences in children. Children's rate of growth is individualistic and depends on biological and external factors such as nutrition and exercise. Therefore, specific guidelines for average height and weight at certain ages or grade level are not provided. The observer may use the child's classroom peers as a comparison group. Please refer to your child development text for supplemental information.

The observer will need to decide upon observable categories of body shape. Staffieri (1967) used the terms mesomorphic, ectomorphic, and endomorphic in his study of children's stereotypes of body shape. Mesomorphic refers to a muscular body shape, ectomorphic indicates a thin body shape, and endomorphic describes a rounded body shape. Other possible categories and definitions may be decided upon and clarified by the observer, perhaps in collaboration with other classmates or colleagues.

An important consideration in children's physical development is the onset of puberty. This profound physical change begins in children during middle childhood, often between the ages of five and nine (Papalia, Olds, & Feldman, 1999.) One of the most observable body changes to occur during puberty for both boys and girls is a rapid height spurt. Other physical changes occurring during puberty include changes in voice, skin texture (i.e., acne), and muscular development. In this strategy, adolescent growth spurt and other physical signs can be noted as observable indications of the onset of puberty (see your child development text).

STRATEGY

3.1 *Observations of Body Growth and Physical Development*

Ages 6–14

Participants: Select several boys and girls from a single age group or from a variety of age groups.

Materials: Clipboard, 1 code sheet for each age group.

Procedure: Complete the codesheet by circling the child's gender as M (male) or F (female). Mark an X on the appropriate line corresponding to the child's estimated height and weight. Indicate the child's ethnicity by marking an X on the appropriate line. Observe males and females from various ethnic groups if possible. Code body shape according to Staffieri's (1967) body shape definitions: "Meso" (mesomorphic), "Ecto" (ectomorphic), or "Endo" (endomorphic). Note an adolescent growth spurt or other physical indicators as sign of puberty.

Record Form 3.1: Observations of Body Growth and Physical Development

Age Group: _____

	Child 1	Child 2	Child 3	Child 4	Child 5
Gender:	M F	M F	M F	M F	M F

Mark an X on the line corresponding to the observed height, weight, and race.

Height:
    Below Ave. _____ _____ _____ _____ _____
    Average _____ _____ _____ _____ _____
    Above Ave. _____ _____ _____ _____ _____

Weight:
    Below Ave. _____ _____ _____ _____ _____
    Average _____ _____ _____ _____ _____
    Above Ave. _____ _____ _____ _____ _____

Ethnicity:
    Caucasian _____ _____ _____ _____ _____
    African Amer. _____ _____ _____ _____ _____
    Hispanic _____ _____ _____ _____ _____
    Asian _____ _____ _____ _____ _____
    Other _____ _____ _____ _____ _____

Body Shape Codes: (Meso, Ecto, Endo)
Body Shape: _____ _____ _____ _____ _____

Indications of Puberty: Adolescent Growth Spurt
        Y N   Y N   Y N   Y N   Y N

Other Indicators of Puberty (list):

    _____ _____ _____ _____ _____

Alternate Coding (body shape)

Use classmates as comparisons and estimate child's height as tall, average, or short, and weight as heavy, medium, or thin. Then code the child's body shape as T/H (tall/heavy), T/M (tall/medium), T/T (tall/thin); or A/T (average/tall), A/M (average/medium), A/T (average/thin); or S/H (short/heavy), S/M (short/medium), S/T (short/thin).

Interpreting Observations

A comprehensive observation of children's growth patterns will likely reveal that they do not continue to grow at as rapid a pace as they did prior to attending elementary school. You may have noticed that many children in the first few years of elementary school begin to slim down and their body trunks begin to lengthen (e.g., Santrock, 1998). You may also have noticed that boys at this age tend to be slightly taller and heavier than girls (Papalia, Olds, & Feldman, 1999). During the later elementary and early middle school years, students may grow a couple of inches each year. This growth pattern continues until puberty (i.e., approximately ages 11–12 for girls; 12–14 for boys), when children again experience a rapid growth in height and changes in their body proportions and form that are related to sexual maturity.

You may find differences in children's growth patterns related to their ethnicity. Researchers have found that a child's ethnicity influences his or her growth (Meredith, 1978). Some researchers have found that ethnicity can be a predictor of physical size and other growth patterns (Ellis, Abrams, & Wong, 1997). You may find that African American children tend to grow faster and may be taller than Caucasian children. You also may find that by age six African American girls tend to be more muscular than Caucasian or Hispanic girls; and that Hispanic girls tend to have a higher percentage of body fat than Caucasian girls of the same height. Clearly these factors need to be considered when evaluating individual children's body growth and development.

Examination of height increases may reveal that girls begin to outdistance boys at approximately age 11 or 12. In general, girls are found to begin to experience body changes associated with puberty about two years earlier than boys (e.g., Meece, 2002). Thus, you may notice physical changes related to puberty about the fifth or sixth grade for girls, and that the accompanying height growth spurt exaggerates height differences between girls and boys. Accordingly, you may have noticed that many boys exhibit a rapid height growth spurt during seventh or eighth grade (i.e., approximately ages 13–14) associated with puberty. It is important to remember that puberty actually begins prior to the development of observable physiological changes and varies individually with children (Papalia, Olds, & Feldman, 1999).

A child's physical size may affect the teacher's and classmates' perceptions of the child, especially if the child is smaller than average or more physically mature than other children in the class. For example, smaller children are sometimes judged as less mature than larger children in the class and are more likely to be retained in a grade than are other larger children (e.g., Meece, 2002). Children who are more physically mature may seek older children for friends who are more similar to them in body shape and development. Teachers who are aware of possible biases in their perceptions of children are better able to make responsible instructional decisions.

——————

Children's Perceptions of Attractiveness

Children as young as eight years old may be concerned about their body shape and their attractiveness to others (Grogan, 1999). Physical attractiveness plays a role in children's self-perceptions and relationships with others. Children's evaluations of their personal appearance and their perceptions about attractiveness to others has been found to influence self-esteem and general psychological well-being (Bennett, 1991; Harter, 1990; Thornton and Ryckman, 1991). Teachers' perceptions of children's attractiveness can influence their treatment of children in the classroom (Algozzine, 1977; Clifford, 1975, Rich 1975). The following interview strategy (Strategy 3.2) can be used to investigate children's general perceptions of attractiveness and various influences on those perceptions.

STRATEGY

3.2   *Perception of Attractiveness Interview*

Appropriate for ages 4–14

Participants: Interview at least 2 girls and 2 boys from the following age groups:

(a) 4–5 (b) 7–9 (c) 12–14.

Materials: Response sheet for each age group.

Procedure: Begin interview by asking the questions listed below. Probe if necessary to elicit expanded answers. Modify terminology for children if necessary (see parentheses). Prompt if children have difficulty responding. Use additional prompts if necessary and continue the questioning using the child's terminology.

Interview Questions

1. Tell me about what you think makes a person look good (attractive).

   Prompt: What makes a person pretty or handsome?

2. Who do you think looks good (attractive)?

   Prompt: Maybe someone on TV or someone you know? Why do you think so?

3. Do you think other people have different ideas about what makes a person look good (attractive)? If so, tell me about what they might think.

Interpreting Responses Observations

You may have observed some differences in the types of responses you obtained from children of different age groups. Younger children may not have appeared as interested in the subject of attractiveness and had much to say, while older children may have appeared very interested in the subject and had much more to say. Younger children likely described attractiveness solely in terms of physical characteristics (i.e., hair color or size) while older children may have included some personality characteristics (e.g., loyal, funny, nice) in their descriptions of attractiveness. Younger children may have provided descriptions that are unrelated to attractiveness (e.g., runs fast, is my friend), and identified an adult (e.g., mother, teacher) as being attractive rather than a peer. Older children more likely identified peers as being attractive (Feldman, Feldman & Goodman, 1988).

Children at all age levels tend to think that attractiveness is related to physical appearance to some extent. You may have found, as did other researchers, that children described slim women or muscular-shouldered men as attractive and tend to dislike obesity (Feldman, Feldman, & Goodman, 1988; Grogan, 1999; Pope, Phillips, & Olivardia, 2000; Staffieri, 1967). Cultural ideals regarding physical appearance also may influence children's descriptions of attractiveness. For example, children in the United States experience a cultural ideal that equates thinness (for women) and muscles (for men) with attractiveness and they are likely to respond accordingly (Feldman, 1998).

Children also tend to identify attractive peers as more popular and they perceive differences in the way teachers treat attractive children in the classroom (Adams, 1980; Feldman, Feldman, & Goodman, 1988). Researchers have found that attractiveness may influence a teacher's academic and social perceptions of children in his or her class-

Record Form 3.2: Children's Perceptions of Attractiveness Response Sheet

Age: _____

1. Tell me about what you think makes a person look good (attractive).

Girl 1:

Girl 2:

Boy 1:

Boy 2:

2. Who do you think looks good (attractive)?

Girl 1:

Girl 2:

Boy 1:

Boy 2:

3. Do you think other people have different ideas about what makes a person look good (attractive)? If so, tell me about what they might think.

Girl 1:

Girl 2:

Boy 1:

Boy 2:

room. Evidence proposed by various researchers suggests that teachers tend to perceive attractive children as being better academic achievers (Cairns & Cairns, 1994; Clifford, 1975) and as having more desirable personality traits (Rich, 1975). Cairns & Cairns specifically found that middle school girls judged unattractive by peers and teachers tended to receive lower grades and were more likely to drop out of school or to become teenage mothers. Educators are encouraged to reflect on their own personal biases related to attractiveness, ascertain the effect of how they treat children in the classroom, and adjust their behavior to be fair and equitable. Another characteristic of children affecting teacher behavior is their activity level.

ACTIVITY LEVEL AND PREFERRED PHYSICAL ACTIVITIES

Children are by nature physically active. There seems to be no question among educators that preschool-age children need play and physical activity to help them develop motor skills. Abundant play and activity breaks are built into good preschool programs. However, the assumption that "play is not learning" may lead some educators to overlook the value of play and physical activity when children enter elementary school. Children may be expected to be quiet and still in order to learn. However, researchers have found that long periods of inactivity tend to reduce children's ability to attend effectively in the classroom, and thus negatively influences children's learning experiences (Pellegrini, 1995; Pellegrini & Smith, 1993).

Daily Activity of Elementary School Children

Physical activity is important for the development of children's motor, cognitive, and social skills (Hinkle, Tuckman, & Sampson, 1993; Tuckman & Hinkle, 1988). As children grow older, their ability to perform the increasingly more complex motor tasks required by school activities becomes integrated with their cognitive and social skills. Opportunities for physical activity and skill practice in school are important for academic progress. The following strategy is designed to reveal children's opportunities for physical activity during their school day.

STRATEGY

Observation of School Day Activity

Ages 5–14

Participants: Observe several children at two or three different age or grade levels.

Procedure: Observe children for approximately 1/2 hour period (longer if possible). Indicate the grade you are observing and record the time of the observation. Mark the gender of the child being observed by circling M or F on the observation sheet.

Record Form 3.3: Observation of School Day Activity

Grades K–8

Observation of School Day Activity

Grade _____

Observation Time _____

Child 1 — Gender M/F			Child 2 — Gender M/F		
Time begin	Time end	Activity	Time begin	Time end	Activity

Record the time (i.e., hour and minute) each time a child engages in physical movement. Record the time the movement ceases. Record the activity (e.g., wiggled in desk, sits still, leaves desk to line up for lunch, leaves classroom) and indicate whether the activity was teacher directed (T) or student-initiated (S).

Alternate Strategy

An observer may wish to prepare anecdotal or running records of a child's activity in the classroom (see Chapter 2).

Interpreting Observations

1. Subtract the time the physical movement begins from the time it ends for each entry. Add the results. How much time did the child spend in physical movement during the time observed?

2. Planned physical movement breaks are those that the teacher directs or that the class engages in as a whole. Note the times of these planned physical movement breaks. Do they occur with any regularity?

You may have noticed that children in lower elementary grades move about the classroom more frequently both with and without teacher permission than do children in upper elementary classrooms. The reason for this is partly biological; the increased myelinization of the nerve endings in older children enables them to control their attention and sit still for longer periods of time than younger children. Therefore, you may have noticed more scheduled activity breaks for younger children. Middle-school/junior high school children have fewer teacher-arranged activity breaks.

The passing periods between classes at the middle/junior high school level help to break up long periods of sitting that can be a negative influence on children's learning and productivity (Pellegrini, 1995). A trend toward longer class sessions (i.e. sessions that meet every other day for twice as long) is becoming common in many schools. Future research will determine if the benefits of longer class periods outweigh the disadvantage of decreased physical movement that can provide refreshment for children's creative thinking processes.

———✂———

Children's Physical Activity Preferences

Children enjoy talking about what they like to do and do not like to do. Educators will be able to encourage children's participation in healthy behavior through exploring children's preferences for various physical activities. Children are naturally curious about the presence of an unfamiliar adult on the playground during recess time. Some children are likely to approach the adult to find out why she or he is there. This may be the perfect opportunity for the observer to "seize the moment" to conduct an impromptu interview to find out what children like to do in their classroom free time, their physical education class, and during recess. (See Chapter 2 for hints on conducting interviews with children and recording responses.) The following interview strategy (Strategy 3.4) may provide some interesting information about children's preferred activities in different school settings.

STRATEGY

Preferred Physical Activities Interview

Ages 4–14

Participants: Interview several children (both boys and girls) from the following age groups: (a) 4–6 (b) 8–10, (c) 12–14.

Materials: Response sheet for each age group interviewed.

Procedure: Begin with the questions listed in the Record Form. Follow up with probes if needed. When coding individual child responses, indicate (M) if child is male and (F) if child is female. Record children's responses in the right margin of the sheet. You may wish to define "free time" activities in order to obtain reliable responses. In general, free-time activities are those activities (games, puzzles, computer, centers, etc.) children participate in when they have completed their classwork assignments or have extra time between lessons. You may need to adapt some of the vocabulary to make it applicable for older children.

Alternate Strategy for Younger Children

You may wish to limit the number of questions for younger children. You could ask questions about only one setting: the classroom, the physical education class, or the playground.

Interpreting Responses and Observations

Children tend to prefer different activities at different ages and these preferences may be related to the preferences of their peers of the same gender (Boulton & Smith, 1993; Thorne, 1993). Children's reports of preferred physical activities will likely conform closely to observations of playaround behavior in Strategy 3.8. Younger children will likely report that they prefer to play on climbing structures and run and chase each other in large open spaces, as Pellegrinis (1995) found. Older children will likely report that their favorite "play" areas are the large open spaces for organized games or shade areas with benches or tables for socializing with friends (Lewis & Phillipsen, 1998; Pellegrini & Smith, 1993). A preference for games with rules also becomes more popular with children as they mature. The rules that govern playground behavior also can impact the type of play that occurs on the playground. Rules that are too stringent may inhibit creative and imaginative play; and rules that are too lax may result in irresponsible and inconsiderate behaviors.

Physical education classes do not often allow for children's free choice of activities. Children at all grade levels are likely to respond that they like playing games in physical education class, especially familiar games that they feel they are likely to win. Least preferred activities in physical education class typically are those that involve structured exercise or running drills. Information about what children like and do not like to do in physical education class can be helpful to the teacher in planning how to integrate needed motor skills practice with preferred activities.

Gender differences in children's activity preferences may have been observed when boys and girls were given free choice of activities on the playground, physical education class, or in the classroom. The largest differences in preferred physical activ-

Record Form 3.4: Preferred Physical Activities Response Sheet

Age level: _____

Classroom Free-Time Activities

1. What are some things you like to do in your classroom when you have free time? Tell me about them.

   Probes: When you do them?

   Who you do them with?

   What are the rules?

2. What are some things your friends like to do during free time in the classroom? Tell me about them.

   Probes: What are some of the different kinds of activities your friends like to do? Do your friends like to do the same kinds of things that you do?

Playground Activities

3. What kinds of activities (games, behaviors) do you like to do on the playground?

   Probes: Tell me about your favorite place to play.

4. Tell me about what you like most about the playground. Why? Who do you play with?

5. Tell me about your playmates on the playground.

   Probes: Only boys or girls or both? Why?

6. Tell me about what your friends like to do on the playground.

   A. What do you do if everyone doesn't want to play the same thing?

7. Tell me about the playground rules.

   Probe: How do the rules affect your play?

8. Tell me about what you would change on the playground.

   Probe: Why is that?

Physical Education Class

9. Tell what you do in physical education class.

   Probes: Tell me about how much time you spend doing each thing. Do you do the same thing each class?

(continued on following page)

(continued from previous page)

10. Tell me about what you like best in physical education class?

    Probes: Tell me more about that.

    Tell me more about why you like it.

    How is it played?

    How many can be involved?

    Is it more fun with more or fewer players?

    Tell me about how much skill you need.

11. Tell me about what you like least to do in physical education class.

    Probes: Why does the teacher have you do those things?

ities may be noticed between younger boys' and older girls' responses. Girls generally prefer less physically active social play in smaller groups, and boys generally prefer active, rough-and-tumble play in large groups (Beneson, 1994; Lever, 1974; Pellegrini, 1990; Pelegrini & Smith, 1993; Richer, 1984; Thorne, 1993). These preferences may be influenced by social and cultural gender role expectations (Alexander & Hines, 1994). However, recent research shows more mixed-gender interactions not only at younger ages, but also in older elementary children (Lewis & Phillipsen, 1998).

Changes suggested by children for playground facilities, activities, physical education classes, and rules in general may be interesting and useful. Sometimes children's ideas may be far-fetched and whimsical, but othertimes they may make sense and could be implemented easily. Listening to children gives adults an opportunity to understand children's perspectives as well as create environments to nurture their growth.

———

MOTOR SKILLS

Children's motor skills continue to develop during childhood (e.g., Meece, 2002; Papalia, Olds, Feldman, 1999; Santrock, 1998). Gross motor skill development involves large muscle movement, and fine motor skill development involves eye-hand and small muscle coordination. Gross and fine motor skills can be observed when the child is active in different school settings. Playgrounds provide opportunities for large muscle development. The classroom provides opportunities for eye-hand and small motor skill development. The structured curriculum in physical education classes also provide opportunities for developing and practicing various motor skills. Research suggests a significant positive association between physical growth and physical performance and between physical performance and cognitive performance (Krombholz, 1997). Thus educators' attention to children's motor skill development is also important for facilitating learning.

Fine Motor Skills

Children's fine motor skills can be observed in many of their daily activities (e.g., dressing, eating, writing, drawing). As children grow older, they develop the ability to use their hands more skillfully and this increased control can be observed in the quality of children's drawing (Caron-Pargue, 1992; Nicholls & Kennedy, 1992; Toomela, 1999) and handwriting (Santrock, 1998). The purpose of the following strategy (Strategy 3.5) is to examine children's drawings and letter production (i.e., signatures) for evidence of the fine motor skills at different ages.

STRATEGY

Observations of Children's Handwriting and Drawing Skills

Ages 4–12

Participants: Select several boys and girls from each of the following age groups: (a) 4–5 years, (b) 6–7 years, (c) 8–9 years, (d) 10–12 years.

Materials: 1–inch square block(s), drawing paper, sharpened pencils.

Procedure: Place small cube(s) on the table in front of the child(ren). Ask child(ren) to draw the block. Then ask child(ren) to write his/their name and age on drawing. (This could be done as a group art project and would enable the observer to obtain a large number of drawing and writing samples at one time.)

The following definitions from Toomela (1999) may help to classify children's drawings into developmental categories.

Scribble: Lines, shapes, or other marks on paper that do not differentiate drawing from other nonrepresentational picture.

Single Unit: Drawing consists of a single unit that represents whole object.

Differentiated Figure: Break down of object into parts; drawing need not look visually realistic, merely needs to include two or more parts of the object.

Integrated Whole: Differentiated parts are reintegrated into visually realistic whole; relationship among parts is realistic.

Interpreting Observations

The development of children's drawing skills follows a progressive pattern that is predictable, universal, and also indicative of emerging abilities in other areas including motor skills, cognition, and socioemotional functioning (Lowenfeld & Brittain, 1982; Malchiodi, 1998; Rubin, 1978; Toomela, 1999). Children's drawings are related to thinking skills (Smith, 1998). Drawing an object involves problem solving for the child to

Record Form 3.5: Drawing and Handwriting Skills Checklist

Age of Child_____
Gender of Child _____

Drawing Skills (check the classification that best describes the drawing of the cube):

1. _____   Scribble

2. _____   Single Unit

3. _____   Differentiated Figure

4. _____   Integrated Whole

Handwriting Skills (check all that apply):

1. _____   Name printed

2. _____   Name printed mostly in upper case letters

3. _____   Some letter reversals

4. _____   Name written in cursive

5. _____   All letters formed correctly

6. _____   Letters uneven size or height

7. _____   Letters too thin or too round

8. _____   Letters written too light or too heavy

9. _____   Letters written shaky or broken

10. _____   Letters uniform size

break down the object into its component parts (i.e., differentiate the object into parts) and then to reconstruct the parts (integrate the parts into a whole) on paper. Although fine motor skills are interrelated with other abilities in the production of a drawing, we will focus only on examining evidence of children's motor skills.

Young children may produce scribble drawings. However, children are generally sufficiently skilled to produce a "Single Unit" drawing of a cube by the age of 4-years (Toomela, 1999). Thus you may have also noticed, as did Toomela, that 4- to 7-year-olds' drawings tended to consist of "Single Unit" drawings—single shapes representing the blocks. The drawings may not resemble the block, but will show a single shape of some kind. Children age 8- to 13-years are more likely to have made a "Differentiated Figure," in which the cube was drawn with two or more of its component subparts included. At this stage, the drawing may not be a visually realistic portrayal of the cube, but the idea of a cube constructed from its parts will be vaguely apparent. You may have only obtained a few drawings classified as "Integrated Whole", as Toomela found this category of drawings characteristic of children and adults over the age of 13 or 14 years. In general, the drawings of elementary school children progress in quality from vague representations to 3-dimensional, realistic drawings. It is important to note that children's drawing skills are heavily influenced by their cognitive abilities (see your child development text).

As with their drawings, four-year-old children's handwriting is also rudimentary, lacking in fine motor control. Gradually letter construction will begin to improve with most letters formed correctly and discriminated by age six. However, you may observe a mixture of upper- and lowercase letters in the printed signature of six-year-olds. By middle childhood you may see further improvement in the basic construction and formation of letters. For example, you may observe that by age seven, children's hand coordination becomes steadier and they are better able to control their writing and drawing instruments. You also will likely see fewer letter reversals and smaller printing (Santrock, 1998). About the age of eight years, children are able to use their hands with greater precision, and thus you will likely observe a shift from printing to cursive writing. Letters will appear to be formed with greater confidence, and decrease in wobbliness and an increase in connectedness may be observed. After age eight, one can expect to see even greater fine motor coordination in children's handwriting. Letter construction gradually becomes smaller and more even sized. By late childhood children's handwriting skills begin to appear more similar to those of adults.

You may have observed from the product samples obtained at each age level that girls seem to outperform boys in fine motor control. In general, girls appear to be better than boys in activities involving fine motor skills. However, boys are usually considered to outperform girls in gross motor skill activities.

—— ✳ ——

Gross Motor Skills

Gross motor skill development generally follows a uniform sequence that is continual and gradual in nature (Meece, 2002). Genetics, cultural expectations and experiences, amount of participation (practice), and activity level are among the factors that have been shown to influence gross motor skill development in children (Cratty, 1986; Feldman, 1998).

Recent research (Goshi et al. 2000) has found that teachers are able to reliably judge children's gross motor skill development by observing children's behavior across school contexts. The purpose of Strategy 3.6 is to assess the sequence of gross motor skill development by observing the behavior displayed by various aged elementary school children in different settings at school (i.e., classroom, physical education class, and playground). Motor skill tasks were adapted from the motor skill test developed by Goshi et al.

STRATEGY

Observation of Gross Motor Skills in School Settings

Ages 4–12

Participants: Select 2 male children and 2 female children from each of the following grades: (a) Pre-K (b) 3rd grade, (c) 6th grade

Materials: One code sheet for each grade, clipboard for code sheet, large and small ball, other materials that can be accessed in the school setting.

Record Form 3.6: Gross Motor Skill Checklist

Age: _____

	Child 1				Child 2			
	M F				M F			
	Observe	Not observe	Success	Not success	Observe	Not observe	Success	Not success
Locomotion								
Hop on one foot								
Able to skip smoothly								
Walk/run smoothly								
Manipulation								
Accurately throw large ball								
Accurately throw small ball								
Catch ball								
Accurately roll ball								
Accurately kick ball								
Stability/Balance								
Balance on one leg								
Walk on balance-type beam								
Dodge ball without falling								
Carry w/out spilling/ dropping								
Body Awareness								
Avoid bumping other children								
Avoid objects when moving in class								
Comfortable talking distance								

Procedure: Mark code sheet with grade and gender of children being observed. Observe each child selected for approximately 15–20 minutes in each of the following settings: classroom, physical education, lunchroom and/or playground. Mark whether the child observed is male or female. Mark an X in the first column (observe) if the skill was demonstrated by the student. In the next two columns mark whether the skill was demonstrated successfully or not successfully. When the observation is over, go back over the checklist and mark any skill not observed.

Alternate Strategy

If only observing in a classroom, one could observe children's body awareness. Locomotion, manipulation, and stability/balance skills are best observed on the playground or in physical education class (you may wish to check with the physical education teacher to find out whether his or her lesson for the day will include any of the listed skills).

Interpreting Observations

You may have observed some developmental differences in gross motor skills between the groups of children. Younger children may have difficulty running fast without tripping, skipping smoothly, or balancing as they walk on a balance-beam type set-up (Cratty, 1986). Younger children also are more accurate at throwing or kicking larger balls than they are with smaller balls. Younger children have more difficulty carrying objects without dropping or spilling and avoiding other bodies and objects when lining up in the classroom.

By the middle grades, children have developed more motor control and are able to demonstrate better control of their body movements. You likely observed that by third grade children are able to run more smoothly, throw and kick more accurately with small balls, and demonstrate more stability than younger children. Third graders also can be expected to demonstrate better body awareness skills enabling them to avoid bumping into other children in lines and when positioning themselves in large groups. The sixth grade children you observed most likely successfully demonstrated all of the gross motor skills indicated on the chart.

You also may have noticed some gender differences. You may have observed that the boys outperformed girls in distance throwing and running. As children approach puberty, gender differences become more salient due to boys' increasing size and strength, cultural gender-role expectations, gender-related experiences, and varying opportunities for practice or participation (Cratty, 1986). With physical development, children's physical performance tends to improve (Krombholtz, 1997). Smoll & Schutz (1990) suggest that as children mature their physical performance is increasing influenced by environmental factors.

———⧓———

PLAYGROUND ACTIVITIES

Ask any grade school child what he or she likes best about school and the response you will likely receive will be either recess or physical education. What is it about these activities that keeps them at the top of children's preferred school activities? More than likely it is the opportunity children have during these activities to move about actively and to interact socially with their peers (Lewis & Phillipsen, 1997; Pellegrini, 1995). Playground recess provides elementary school children with needed breaks from sedentary classroom activities and with opportunities for exercise.

Playground recess also provides elementary school children with the opportunity for social interactions (Lewis & Phillipsen, 1997). Recess behaviors have been linked to children's social competence (Pellegrini, 1990). The successful adaptation to school requires developing the ability to get along with others and the playground provides a wonderful opportunity to practice necessary skills.

School children are not the only ones interested in playground activities. Educators are becoming increasingly aware of the important educational implications of physical activity, exercise, and social interaction that occurs on the playground and the necessity of providing children opportunities for play (Pellegrini, 1995).

Playground Environment and Play Opportunities

Playgrounds are supposed to be fun, safe places to encourage exercise and creative play in children (Brett, Moore, & Provenzo, 1993). Just as we plan curriculum to help children progress in academic subjects, we can give thoughtful care and planning to children's play areas to assure they will encourage children's development.

The following observation strategy (Strategy 3.7) uses a checklist/rating scale system to examine children's playgrounds in terms of the types of play areas opportunities provided, their complexity and appeal, and their safety features. The checklist/rating scale is adapted from the Playground Rating System developed by Joe Frost (Frost & Klein, 1979).

STRATEGY

3.7   *Playground Environment Checklist/Rating Scale*

Materials: Clipboard and code sheet for each playground.

Procedure: Observe at least 2 playgrounds that differ in population served (e.g., primary school vs. middle school), geographic location (e.g., rural vs. city), or amount of variation in play or creative opportunity (e.g., traditional vs. creative playgrounds). For Sections I, II, and III, mark items observed about the playground with an X. For Sections IV and V, circle the choice that best describes the playground.

Interpreting Observations

Different types of playgrounds encourage different types of play behaviors (Frost and Campbell, 1985, Hayward, Rothenberg, & Beasley, 1974). If you observed swings, slides, and other climbing equipment constructed of steel and permanently set in the ground, it is likely you are on a traditional playground. Most American playgrounds are

Record Form 3.7: Playground Environment Checklist/Rating Scale

Section I. Play Areas

1. _____ A hard surface area with space for games.

2. _____ Play equipment available (i.e., Balls, jump ropes, bases, etc.)

3. _____ Equipment for active play

   _____ Slide(s)

   _____ Swing(s)

   _____ Climbing structure(s)

4. _____ Ample space for various types of large-muscle exercise & movement

5. _____ Equipment to encourage balance, coordination, and strength (i.e., Low Balance beam, chinning bars, etc.

6. _____ Grass area for chasing or organized games

7. _____ Sand play area and equipment to support sand play

8. _____ Water play area and equipment to support water play

9. _____ Structures for creative play (house, boat, car, etc.)

10. _____ Stage area for dramatic play

11. _____ Natural area that can attract birds, butterflies, bugs, etc.

12. _____ Garden area and tools

13. _____ Shade areas

14. _____ Area with tables/benches

15. _____ Area for social interaction with peers

Section II. Playground Safety

1. _____ Protective fence separating hazardous areas

2. _____ Shock-absorbing surfacing material under all climbing and moving equipment (e.g., sand, wood chips, shredded tire, etc.)

3. _____ Equipment matched to size of children (i.e., small equipment for younger, smaller students, etc.)

4. _____ Play area clean and free of litter, broken glass, etc.

5. _____ Equipment free of sharp edges, with no broken parts, in good repair

6. _____ Children within eyesight of playground monitors

(continued on following page)

(continued from previous page)

Section III. Type of Play Opportunities

(In other words, what can you expect to see children doing on this playground?)

1. _____ Encourages play; is inviting with easy access

2. _____ Promotes creativity with versatile equipment

3. _____ Encourages socializing

4. _____ Provides graduated challenges to foster physical development (e.g., obstacle course, chin-up bars, balance bar, etc.)

5. _____ Promotes various types of play (i.e., functional, constructive, dramatic, organized with rules)

6. _____ Equipment is movable to conform to children's creative play

7. _____ Playground is accessible for children with disabilities

Section IV. Complexity of Playground Equipment

Rate the complexity of the playground equipment on the scale following the item by circling the number that best describes the complexity of the equipment.

Swing(s)

(1) single swing set, simple sling- seat swing(s), all same size

(2) multiple swing sets, limited size variation

Slide(s)

(1) single slide, low height

(2) multiple slides, various heights

(3) multiple slides, various heights, widths, and shapes

Climbing structure(s)

(1) simple structure, one level, one climbing surface

(2) more complex structure, multiple levels OR more than one climbing surface

(3) most complex structure, multiple levels AND multiple climbing surfaces

Creative play structure(s)

(1) single play structure, one-dimensional play focus (e.g., row boat with seats)

(2) single play structure, multidimensional play focus (e.g., row boat with seats and bell)

(3) single or multiple play structures, with multidimensional play focus and multiple play areas (e.g., multiple deck ship, ladders between floors, seats, bell, steering wheel, slide off back)

(continued on following page)

(continued from previous page)

Section V. Playground Appeal

Circle the number that best describes the general appeal of the playground according to the following criteria.

Functionality of Playground Equipment (i.e., supports and encourages play and exercise)

(1) does not meet expected function

(2) meets expected function

(3) exceeds expected function

Comfort level of equipment and general area

(1) metal equipment, asphalt, limited space

(2) metal equipment, grass area

(3) non-metal equipment, grass area, tables/benches, shade

Aesthetic (visual appeal)

(1) drab, dull, uninteresting

(2) colorful, interesting

(3) bright, stimulating

Creative

(1) limited in type(s) of creative play encouraged

(2) encourages various types of creative play but opportunities limited to children at single age or level of motor skill development

(3) encourages various types of creative play in children at various ages and levels of motor skill development

of the traditional type (Brett, Moore, & Provenzo, 1993). While functional for younger children's gross motor exercise needs, this type of playground is least likely to encourage creative or imaginative play. Playgrounds that are designed to include equipment made from railroad ties, rubber tires, telephone poles, and other materials often encourage a wider range of creative play.

Playgrounds with a variety of play areas provide more opportunities for children to use their imagination and creativity, and better suit a wide age range of children. Younger children like to engage in physical activity on the playground. As children grow older, their peers become important factors in playground activities, so playgrounds need to accommodate children's growing need for group and social activities.

Safety is an issue on every playground. You likely observed some type of shock-absorbing material under climbing and moving equipment, and a safety fence separating the playground from a road or other dangerous area. On playgrounds used by young elementary children, you may have observed some smaller-sized equipment (e.g., small slides, small swing seats). Playgrounds used by children with disabilities often include adaptations that provide increased access. Refer to Brett, Moore, and Provenzo (1993) for suggestions in planning or adapting playground environments (see Resources).

Children's Playground Behaviors

A small amount of research has been conducted to investigate children's playground behavior. The research evidence that is available suggests that playground behavior is related to positive cognitive and social outcomes for children (Brett, Moore, & Provenzo, 1993; Pellegrini, 1995). Pellegrini (1984, 1987) found recess behavior to be related to children's ability to solve hypothetical social problems. The playground is an important place for children to learn the social skills and strategies necessary for later development. The "play" atmosphere of the playground context is unique in that it allows children to experiment with different social strategies in a relatively safe environment. Opportunities for play enhance children's cognitive, social-emotional, psychomotor development in an integrated fashion.

The following observation strategy (Strategy 3.8) is focused on investigating the various types of playground behaviors demonstrated by children at different ages. Prior to completing the following strategy, it will be important for observers to clearly define the behaviors being investigated (see Chapter 2).

STRATEGY

Observation of Playground Behaviors

Ages 4–12

Participants: Select several children (boys *and* girls) from each of the following age groups: (a) 4–6 (b) 8–9 (c) 11–12.

Materials: Stopwatch, clipboard, category descriptions, and three code sheets.

Procedure: Observe a selected child for one minute, assign his/her behavior to the appropriate categories on a code sheet like the one shown below by making a checkmark in the appropriate space. Follow the same procedure for each of the other three children selected. Repeat the procedure for each age group until you have observed each of the selected children for five minutes.

The following definitions may be helpful:

Active Play: Play characterized by lively movement (e.g., running, climbing, throwing, kicking, etc.) and/or logical thinking.

Vigorous: Energetic, forceful play.

Rough and tumble: Horseplay, wrestling.

Games with rules: Players compete with each other to succeed in game that is governed by strict set of rules (e.g., football, baseball, four-square, checkers).

Passive Play: play characterized by quiet behaviors with little or no physical movement.

Adult-Directed Attention: Child's behavior is directed toward seeking adult attention

Observer-Directed Attention: Child's behavior is directed toward seeking the observer's attention.

Record Form 3.8: Observation of Playground Behaviors

Age group: _____

Observation: 1   2   3   4   5

Date: _____

	Child 1	Child 2	Child 3	Child 4
Gender:	M F	M F	M F	M F
Size of Group (#)	_____	_____	_____	_____
Physical Level of Behavior				
Active play				
Vigorous	_____	_____	_____	_____
Rough and tumble	_____	_____	_____	_____
Games with rules	_____	_____	_____	_____
Passive play				
Talking	_____	_____	_____	_____
Walking	_____	_____	_____	_____
Sitting	_____	_____	_____	_____
Waiting	_____	_____	_____	_____
Solitary active play	_____	_____	_____	_____
Solitary passive play	_____	_____	_____	_____
Play w/same gender peer(s)	_____	_____	_____	_____
Play w/opposite gender peer(s)	_____	_____	_____	_____
Location of child				
Swing area	_____	_____	_____	_____
Slides	_____	_____	_____	_____
Jungle gym	_____	_____	_____	_____
Hard surface area	_____	_____	_____	_____
Grass/field area	_____	_____	_____	_____
Other (describe)	_____	_____	_____	_____
Adult-directed attention	_____	_____	_____	_____
Observer-directed attention	_____	_____	_____	_____

Interpreting Observations

One purpose of this observation is to increase educators' awareness of the various physical activities demonstrated by children of different grade levels and genders. You may have noticed that boys and girls choose to play in different parts of the playground and that their play behavior is often different. If you found that boys seem to be more active on the playground than girls, your results will be in agreement with other researchers' findings (e.g., Humphreys & Smith, 1984; Lewis & Phillipsen, 1998; Maccoby & Jacklin, 1987). Boys also tend to demonstrate higher frequencies of rough and tumble or physically vigorous play that is characterized by running, chasing, jumping on, and play fighting (Pellegrini, 1995).

You also may have observed as Lewis and Phillipsen (1998) that older children tended to play in larger, same-gender groups more than did younger children. In contrast, other researchers have found that younger children are more likely to play in same-gender groups than older children (Csikszentmihalyi & Larsen, 1984; Feiring & Lewis, 1991; Luria & Herzog, 1991; Maccoby, 1988). Thorne (1993) observed that most mixed-gender play among younger children occurred in large group chase games (i.e., tag). Lewis & Phillipsen (1998) indicate that older children tend to play games with rules in large groups more frequently than do younger children.

You also may have noticed that children choose to play in different parts of the playground and that play behaviors are different from area to area. Elementary school children are in various stages of motor skill development and they appear to choose play activities accordingly. Lewis and Phillipsen (1998) found that large, open play yards were popular with all ages and genders of children. Open play yards with soft grassy surfaces encourage children to exercise large muscles in rough and tumble play activities (Pellegrini, 1995). Open play yards encourage older children to play organized games requiring space for movement. Jungle gyms and slides are more popular for younger children, with girls preferring the jungle gyms and boys spending more time on the slides. Hard court surfaces for boys' game playing and tree areas for girls' socializing are most popular with older children. These results emphasize the importance of providing a variety of play structures and playground areas for children of differing ages and genders. Inviting play and recreation areas will encourage healthy behavior.

———※※※———

CHILDREN'S HEALTH ISSUES

Children's understanding of general health issues is important for healthy behavior (Olvera-Ezzell, Power, & Cousins, 1990). Children's healthy behavior can facilitate school success (Tinsley, 1992). Health problems may have a negative effect on all aspects of children's physical, cognitive, and social, emotional development. Health knowledge is an essential tool for promoting children's healthy behavior practices. Strategy 3.9 provides an interview that can be used with the school nurse or other school personnel to investigate the health concerns of elementary school children. The issue of confidentiality is important to consider in this type of interview. The nurse can be informed prior to the interview that you do not wish to know names or specific information regarding individual children. (See Chapter 2 for information regarding confidentiality.)

STRATEGY

3.9 Visit with the School Nurse

Participants: School nurse

Materials: Interview questions, Notebook

Procedure: Interview a school nurse using the questions listed below.

Note: The entire interview may be a lengthy process and may require up to an hour or more of the nurse's time. You may wish to ask the nurse how much time is available for the interview and, if necessary, prioritize your questions by choosing the ones most important to you. It also may be helpful to provide the nurse with a copy of the interview questions in advance so he/she may be prepared for your questions. The nurse also may have a preference for specific questions he or she feels may be most informative and helpful.

Questions

1. Tell me about your job as school nurse. What are the ages (grades) of the children you work with?

2. Tell me about some of the reasons children seek medical attention.

3. Tell me about the most common types of injuries children suffer in physical education or on the playground. Do any types of injuries appear to be more common at any specific grade level? Why are these more common?

4. What types of illnesses are most common? Is any one type of illness or complaint more common to specific grades than others?

5. Tell me about the different ways children describe their complaints. What differences do you see at various grades in how children are able to articulate their meanings? Are there developmental differences in the way children talk about their health that teachers need to consider?

6. What guidelines do you suggest for when to send a child to see the nurse?

7. Tell me in a general way about the medication needs of children in your school building. What should teachers know about the medications children in their classroom are taking? Tell me about any other reason besides medication, injuries, and illness that teachers might seek your help relative to children's health issues?

8. What do you think is important for teachers to know about children's health needs, including sleep and diet needs? Are there any signs or symptoms to look for?

9. What general suggestions about children's health do you have for teachers and other educators?

Alternate Strategy

Due to the length of this strategy students may wish to work as a group and divide the interview into sections along common themes (e.g., common illnesses, injuries, health information needs). Students could work together as a group, with individuals obtaining responses to different interview questions. Then students could combine their responses to complete an entire interview. Classroom teachers or school office staff also may be helpful respondents for gathering information about children's health issues. Interesting comparisons may be made between nurses from different regions (rural vs. urban) or at different grade levels (primary vs. middle school vs. junior high).

Interpreting Responses and Observations

The interview with the nurse can provide information about children's everyday health concerns. You will likely obtain responses reflecting the nurse's role in the treatment of playground and physical education class injuries and caring for headaches, fevers, sore throats, and stomachaches. The nurse also can provide guidelines concerning which complaints warrant a visit to the nurse and which complaints can be handled in the classroom. Knowledge concerning the symptoms to look for before sending a child to the nurse can eliminate lost learning time for children. The nurse also may be able to help the educator understand the difficulty children may have in describing their health complaints. You may have found that the nurse reports that young children have more difficulty describing exactly where they hurt when they are feeling sick. Young children often need help in expressing their feelings about sickness (Papalia, Olds, & Feldman, 1999; Parcel, 1979). However, older children with expressive language difficulty also may have trouble describing their symptoms as well.

Elementary school children are expected to make important choices concerning major health issues. Enhancing children's health knowledge provides them with the information needed to help them make informed decisions about their behavior. Current literature on school children's health suggests that the most effective approach in addressing children's overall health needs is to help children learn to make responsible health choices (Payton et al., 2000). An understanding educator can also provide support for children to make responsible health choices by providing a school environment in which children feel supported, cared about, and connected (e.g., Eccles & Barber, 1999; Meece, 2002; Resnick et al., 1997).

———✳✳✳———

CHAPTER SUMMARY

Educators are expected to increase their knowledge of children's physical development and to improve their understanding of children's perceptions, attitudes, and behaviors related to physical development. Observation and interview strategies are used to investigate similarities and differences in children's physical growth and skill development that are demonstrated in elementary school classrooms and on playgrounds. It is expected that educators' increased awareness of children's physical needs and preferences will result in the encouragement of children's healthy attitudes and behaviors. The importance of the playground as a setting for motor skill development and practice is stressed. Educators' responsiveness to children's physical needs and increased knowledge regarding how physical activity can be used to facilitate children's learning will enable them to foster children's healthy physical growth at school, and their cognitive and social functioning as well.

REFLECTION QUESTIONS

1. How could a child's physical size influence his or her school performance, behavior or social relationships? How might this affect a teacher's perception of the child's ability? (Strategy 3.1)

2. How might children's feelings about their own attractiveness affect their perceptions of teacher and peer acceptance? How could a teacher encourage children's acceptance of their body shape and appearance, and encourage them to use their physical skills? (Strategy 3.2)

3. How can a teacher determine whether a child's out of seat behavior is related to physical need or just misbehavior? What other factors might be responsible for out of seat behavior? (Strategy 3.3)

4. How could a teacher use information about children's activity preferences to facilitate classroom instruction, encourage children's social relationships, and/or increase motivation? (Strategy 3.4)

5. How might educators use information about children's motor skills to improve instructional activities? (Strategies 3.5, 3.6, 3.8)

6. How can educators use Strategies 3.7 and 3.8 to promote children's physical, socioemotional, and cognitive abilities?

7. How might children's awareness of health issues promote their healthy behavior? (Strategy 3.9)

8. How could Strategies 3.2 and 3.9 be used to identify specific health issues at school?

RESOURCES

Brett, A., Moore, R. C., & Provenzo, E. F. Jr.(1993). *The complete playground book*. Syracuse, NY: Syracuse University Press.

Cratty, B. J. (1986). *Perceptual and motor development in infants and children,* 3rd ed. Englewood Cliffs, NJ: Prentice Hall.

Pellegrini, A. D. (1995). *School recess and playground behavior: Educational and developmental roles*. Albany: State University of New York Press.

TIPS FOR TEACHERS

This chapter provided a number of ways for classroom teachers to gather specific information concerning children's physical growth and development in school. Strategy 3.1 can be adapted to provide a more comprehensive record of individual student growth by recording children's actual height and weight at the beginning, middle, and end of the school year. This strategy could be enhanced with snapshots of the children taken at the same times. Group photographs of the class, with children arranged in the same order each time, would provide interesting documentation of individual child growth as well as variation in growth throughout the classroom during the school year.

The interview questions in Strategies 3.2 and 3.4 can be used to provide the teacher with information that could be useful in guiding his or her instructional practice in the classroom. The Perceptions of Attractiveness Interview (Strategy 3.2) could be adapted and used for small or large group discussion as a lesson in a science, health, or nutrition curriculum. This interview could be used as an introductory discussion related to more specific health concerns such as eating disorders. Children's Preferred Physical Activities Interview (Strategy 3.4) could be used to assist the teacher in determining motivational strategies to be used during the school year.

Teachers in the early elementary grades may wish to maintain a collection of children's handwriting samples to document student progress in the development of their fine motor skills throughout the school year. Strategy 3.5 can be adapted for routine use in the classroom by having children print or write the alphabet letters, or sentences containing many commonly used letters. The same exercise can be used repeatedly during the course of the school year to document improvement, specifically in children's handwriting development.

Teachers' observations of children's gross motor skills (Strategy 3.6) could be used as a beginning of the year exercise to check the level of skill demonstrated by individuals in the classroom and the classroom as a whole. Children's playground behaviors (Strategy 3.8) can provide teachers with information regarding how children in the class tend to group themselves. These naturally occurring groups can be used when cohesiveness is needed to facilitate instructional activities. At other times the groups can be separated and teacher support provided to encourage children to build relationships and learn with other classmates (see Chapter 5).

References

Adams, G. R. (1980). The effects of physical attractiveness on the socialization process. In G. W. Lucker, K. A. Ribbens, and J. A. McNamara (Eds.), *Psychological aspects of facial form (Monographs 11, Craniofacial Growth Series)*. Ann Arbor: Center for Human Growth and Development, University of Michigan.

Alexander, G. M., and Hines, M. (1994). Gender labels and play styles: The relative contribution to children's selection of playmates. *Child Development, 65,* 869–879.

Algozzine, O. (1977). Perceived attractiveness and classroom interactions. *Journal of Experimental Education, 46,* 63–66.

Benenson, J. F., (1994). Ages four to six years: Changes in the structures of play networks of girls and boys. *Merrill-Palmer Quarterly, 40,* 478 –487.

Bennett, K. (1991). *Adult body image.* Nottingham: University of Nottingham.

Berlyne, D. (1966). Curiosity and exploration. *Science, 153,* 25–33.

Boulton, M. J., and Smith, P. K. (1993). Ethnic gender partner, and activity preferences in mixed-race schools in the U.K.: Playground observations. In C. H. Hart (Ed.), *Children on playgrounds.* Albany, NY: State University of New York Press.

Brett, A., Moore, R. C., and Provenzo, E. F., Jr. (1993). *The complete playground book.* Syracuse, NY: Syracuse University Press.

Cairns, R. B., and Cairns, B. D. (1994). *Lifelines and risks: Pathways of youth in our time.* Cambridge, England: Cambridge University Press.

Caron-Pargue, J. (1992). A functional analysis of decomposition and integration in children's cylinder drawings. *British Journal of Developmental Psychology, 10*, 51–69.

Clifford, M. M. (1975). Physical attractiveness and academic performance. *Child Study Journal, 5*, 201–209.

Cratty, B. J. (1986). *Perceptual and motor development in infants and children,* 3rd ed. Englewood Cliffs, NJ: Prentice Hall.

Csikszentmihalyi, M., and Larson, R. (1984). *Being adolescent.* New York: Basic Books.

Eccles, J. S., and Barber, B. S. (1999). Student council, volunteering, basketball, or marching band: What kind of extracurricular involvement matters? *Journal of Adolescent Research, 14*(1), 10–43.

Ellis, K. J., Abrams, S. A., and Wong, W. W. (1997). Body composition of a young multiethnic female population. *American Journal of Clinical Nutrition, 65*, 724–731.

Feiring, C., and Lewis, M. (1991). The development of social networks from early to middle childhood: Gender differences and the relation to school competence. *Sex Roles, 25*, 237–253.

Feldman, R. S. (1998). *Child Development.* Upper Saddle River, NJ: Prentice Hall.

Feldman, W., Feldman, E., and Goodman, J. T. (1988). Culture versus biology: Children's attitudes toward thinness and fatness. *Pediatrics, 81*, 190–194.

Frost, J. L., and Campbell, S. (1985). The effects of playground type on the cognitive and social play behaviors of grade two children. In J. L. Frost and S. Sunderlin (Eds.), *When children play.* Wheaton, MD: ACEI.

Frost, J. L. and Klein, B. L. (1979). *Children's Play & Playgrounds.* Boston, MA: Allyn & Bacon.

Fugaro, R. A. L. (1985). *A manual of sequential art activities for classified children and adolescents.* Springfield, IL: Charles C. Thomas.

Gallahue, D. L. (1989). *Understanding motor development: Infants, children, adolescents,* 2nd ed. Indianapolis, IN: Benchmark Press.

Goshi, F., Demura, S., Kasuga, K., Sato, S., and Minami, M. (2000). Use of subjective estimation in motor skill tests of young children: Judgment based on observation of behavior in daily life. *Perceptual and Motor Skills, 90*, 215–226.

Grogan, S. (1999). *Body image.* New York: Routledge.

Hart, C. (1993). *Children on playgrounds.* Albany, NY: SUNY Press.

Harter, S. (1990). Self and identity development. In S. S. Feldman and G.R. Elliott (Eds.), *At the threshold: The developing adolescent.* Cambridge, MA: Harvard University Press.

Hayward, G., Rothenberg, M., and Beasley, R. (1974). Children's play and urban playground environments: A comparison of traditional, contemporary, and adventure types. *Environment and Behavior, 6*, 131–168.

Hinkle, J. S., Tuckman, B. W., and Sampson, J. P. (1993). The psychology, physiology and creativity of middle school aerobic exercises. *Elementary School Guidance and Counseling, 28*(2), 133–145.

Hughes, F. P., Noppe, L. D., and Noppe, I. C. (1996). *Child development.* Upper Saddle River, NJ: Prentice Hall.

Humphreys, A. P., and Smith, P. K. (1984). Rough-and-tumble in preschool and playground. In P. K. Smith (Ed.), *Play in animals and humans.* Oxford: Blackwell.

Krombholz, H. (1997). Physical performance in relation to age, sex, social class and sports activities in kindergarten and elementary school. *Perceptual and Motor Skills, 84,* 1168–1170.

Lever, J. (1974). Sex differences in the games children play. *Social Problems, 23,* 478–487.

Lewis, T. E., and Phillipsen, L. C. (1998). Interactions on an elementary school playground: Variations by age, gender, race, group size, and playground area. *Child Study Journal, 28*(4), 309–320.

Lowenfeld, V., and Brittain, W. L. (1982). *Creative and mental growth.* London: Collier MacMillan.

Luria, Z., and Herzog, E. W. (1991). Sorting gender out in a children's museum. *Gender and Society, 5,* 224–232.

Maccoby, E. E. (1988). Gender as a social category. *Developmental Psychology, 24,* 755–765.

Maccoby, E. E., and Jacklin, C. N. (1987). Gender segregation in childhood. In H. W. Reese (Ed.), *Advances in child development and behavior* (Vol. 20, pp. 239–288). New York: Academic Press.

Malchiodi, C. A. (1998). *Understanding children's drawings.* New York: The Guilford Press.

Meece, J. (2002*). Child and Adolescent Development for Educators,* 2nd ed. Boston, MA: McGraw-Hill.

Meredith, H. (1978). Research between 1960 and 1970 on the standing height of young children in different parts of the world. In H. W. Reese and L. P. Lipsitt (Eds.), *Advances in child development and behavior* (Vol. 12). New York: Academic Press.

Nicholls, A. L., and Kennedy, J. M. (1992). Drawing development: From similarity of features to direction. *Child Development, 63,* 227–241.

Olvera-Ezzell, N., Power, T. G., and Cousins, J. H. (1990). Maternal socialization of children's eating habits: Strategies used by obese Mexican-American mothers. *Child Development, 61,* 395–400.

Papalia, D. E., Olds, S. W., and Feldman, R. D. (1999). *A child's world: Infancy through adolescence.* Boston: McGraw-Hill.

Parcel, G. S., Tiernan, K., Nadar, P. R., and Gottlob, D. (1979). Health education and kindergarten children. *Journal of School Health, 57,* 150–156.

Payton, J. W., Wardlaw, D. M., Graczyk, P. A., Bloodworth, M. R., Tompsett, C. J., and Weissberg, R. P. (2000). Social and emotional learning: A framework for promoting mental health and reducing risk behaviors in children and youth. *Journal of School Health, 70*(5), 179–185.

Pellegrini, A. (1984). The social-cognitive ecology of pre-school classrooms. *International Journal of Behavioral Development, 7,* 321–332.

Pellegrini, A. (1987). Rough-and-tumble play: Developmental and educational significance. *Educational Psychologist, 22,* 23–43.

Pellegrini, A. D. (1990). Elementary school children's playground behavior: Implications for children's social-cognitive development. *Children's Environments Quarterly, 7,* 8–16.

Pellegrini, A. D., and Smith, P. K. (1993). School recess: Implications for educatoin and development. *Review of Educational Research, 63,* 51–67.

Pope, H. G., Jr., Phillips, K. A., and Olivardia, R. (2000). *The Adonis complex: The secret crisis of male body obsession.* New York: The Free Press.

Resnick, M. D., Bearman, P. S., Blum, R. W., Bauman, K. E., Harris, K. M., Jones, J., Tabor, J., Beuhring, T., Sieving, R. E., Shew, M., Ireland, M., Bearinger, L. H., and Udry, J. R. (1997). Protecting adolescents from harm: Findings from the national longitudinal study on adolescent health. *JAMA: Journal of the American Medical Association, 278*(10), 823–832.

Rich, J. (1975). Effects of children's physical attractiveness on teacher's evaluation. *Journal of Educational Psychology, 67,* 599–609.

Richer, S. (1984). Sexual inequality and children's play. *Canadian Review of Sociology and Anthropology, 21,* 166–180.

Rubin, J. A. (1978). *Child art therapy: Understanding and helping children grow through art.* New York: Van Nostrand Reinhold.

Santrock, J. W. (1998). *Child Development,* 8th ed. Boston, MA: McGraw-Hill.

Smith, N. R. (1998). *Observation drawing with children: A framework for teachers.* New York: Teachers College Press.

Smoll, F. L., and Schutz, R. W. (1990). Quantifying gender differences in physical performance: A developmental perspective. *Developmental Psychology, 26*(3), 360–369.

Staffieri, J. R. (1967). A study of social stereotypes of body image in children. *Journal of Personality and Social Psychology, 7,* 101–104.

Thorne, B. (1993). *Gender play: Girls and boys in school.* New Brunswick, NJ: Rutgers University Press.

Thornton, B., and Ryckman, R. M. (1991). Relationship between physical attractiveness, physical effectiveness, and self-esteem: A cross-sectional analysis among adolescents. *Journal of Adolescence, 14,* 85–98.

Tinsley, B. (1992). Multiple influences of the acquisition and socialization of children's health attitudes and behavior: An integrative review. *Child Development, 63,* 1043–1069.

Toomela, A. (1999). Drawing development: Stages in the representation of a cube and a cylinder. *Child Development, 70*(5), 1141–1150.

Tuckman, B. W., and Hinkle, J. S. (1988). An experimental study of the physical and psychological effects of aerobic exercise on school children. In B. G. Melamed, K. A. Matthews, D. K. Routh, B. Stabler, and N. Schneiderman (Eds.), *Child health psychology.* Hillsdale, NJ: Erlbaum.

Cognitive Development

CHAPTER PREVIEW

This chapter is intended to provide child study students and educators with strategies to assist with entering the minds of children and making connections to a variety of cognitive development theories and research described in child development texts. It includes observations of cognitive processes revealed in play and behavior in everyday activities as well as in structured tasks. Interviews with teachers and observations of school activities are included to provide opportunities for further reflection on how belief systems and settings may influence students' cognitive development and learning.

THINKING IN PLAY

Virtually all major developmental theorists attest to the value of play in fostering children's cognitive development (e.g., Piaget, 1926; Vygotsky, 1978). In Chapter 5, opportunities for observing the functions of play for socioemotional development are provided; in this chapter, the focus is on observing children's cognitive processes at work during everyday spontaneous and structured play activities. Strategy 4.1 provides opportunities to look at how children learn and practice using symbols (e.g., language) and rules, solve problems, and communicate with others within a variety of play settings. Strategy 4.2 allows for focused observations on how adults and peers guide play activities, and the competencies children demonstrate in their guidance roles. It may be necessary to review definitions of cognitive processes provided in your child development text before proceeding with the strategies (perhaps in discussion with fellow students and the instructor).

STRATEGY

4.1

Observation of Cognitive Processes Revealed in Play

Ages 4–10

Participants: Target two children from two of the following age groups: (a) 4–5 years, (b) 6–8 years, (c) 9–10 years

Procedure: Observe during all "free-choice" or "play" times in two settings: (a) classroom, (b) home, (c) playground, or (d) other recreational setting.

Step 1: Observe two or more children participating together in a play activity for 15–20 minutes. Record the actual behavior and words of the two target children. Attempt to capture exact words whenever possible, as well as emotional expressions (see Chapter 2 for suggestions on writing running records). This observation may be conducted with a partner who concentrates on recording the behavior of one of the target children.

Step 2: Rewrite the observation from your raw notes (Step 1), providing enough detail so that an outside reader can visualize the interactions and activities, and leaving space in the margins to write your interpretations, reflections, and cognitive process categories.

Step 3: Examine the revised observation for evidence of cognitive processes and competencies demonstrated across age groups. For example, you may have observed evidence of the following potential cognitive benefits of play:

> Pretend/symbolic/imaginative play (flexibility of thought)
> Use of vocabulary/language (complexity)
> Understanding of game rules
> Perspective/role-taking
> Communication/problem-solving with others
> Problem-solving with materials
> Focused concentration

Step 4: Taking care to support each of your points with excerpts of behavior or words from your actual observations, write a report based on your analysis of children's cognitive processes revealed in play. You may want to organize the report by comparing how children of different ages in your sample demonstrated particular cognitive processes or competencies (selecting a few from the list above).

Interpreting Observations

Compare your observations of cognitive processes revealed in play behavior to developmental trends described in your child development text. For example, you may have noted that children ages 4–5 demonstrated much imaginative/symbolic thinking in dramatic or social pretend play, and that older children appeared to focus on understanding and communicating about the rules of games. Competencies in game-playing and rule-understanding continue to develop in elementary-age children (e.g., Piaget, 1932/1965; Thorne, 1993).

You also may have observed some age-related differences in children's spoken language, especially between the 4– and 6–7–year-old children. For example, you may have noted increases in their use of lengthy complex sentences; their use of vocabulary; and their ability to converse with others (demonstrate perspective-taking).

In addition, you also may have observed differences in the types or quality of cognitive skills demonstrated in play across activity settings. For example, children may have different opportunities to engage in and demonstrate competencies in imaginative or constructive play (e.g., exploration with science materials, computers; writing imaginative stories; performing plays) in the classroom and at home.

The following strategy allows the observer to focus on peer collaboration or guided participation during play activities. In particular, observers are asked to attend to children's developing cognitive skills as collaborators or peer tutors ("child teachers"). (See your child development text for a full discussion of guided participation.) Children's skills in this area are important for educators to consider today in light of theory and research supporting the value of peer collaboration in academic learning (see Rogoff, 1998, 1990; Vygotsky, 1978).

STRATEGY

4.2 *Guided Participation Game: Play with Peers and Adults*

Ages 5–adult

Participants: Observe the following dyads: (a) "child teacher" (age 5–9) with a less skilled/experienced child, (b) "child teacher" (age 10–14) with less skilled/experienced child, (c) adult with child.

Materials: Board, construction (e.g., legos), or computer game.

Procedure: Ask the "child teachers" to explain how to play the game or construct an object (according to a model) to another child who is either less familiar or less skilled at playing. Record the explanations, hints, gestures, and responses of the "child teacher" as well as their partners' questions, reactions, and behaviors demonstrating effectiveness at playing the game (e.g., correct moves). Repeat the procedure observing an adult (who knows how to play) assist a child with playing a similar game. End each session by helping the child participants successfully play a game.

Recording and Interpreting Observations

First, prepare running records of the interactions observed during game playing (see Chapter 2). Then, examine your records for evidence of effective and ineffective attempts at guiding the learner. For example, you may note whether the child and adult "teachers" used guidance techniques, such as (1) explaining the goals of the game or task, (2) discussing strategies or ways to meet the goals, (3) involving the "learners" in the discussion, (4) providing cues rather than always telling exactly what to do, and (5) providing appropriate hints that help the learner understand the task. You may want to organize your observation notes in the following way to prepare for writing an analysis.

For Each Observation:

I. Describe child/adult "teacher" or guide (specify age and expertise) and setting.

II. Describe types of guidance attempts made by the "teacher" (e.g., explains goals, discusses strategies, provides hints and cues, commands). Refer to exact quotes and observations of behavior.

III. Describe the effectiveness of guidance attempts in terms of the "learner's" responses (e.g., words, game moves) and apparent understanding of the game rules.

Summary Analysis

Compare and contrast interactions of the three dyads. Relate your observations when appropriate to research on guided participation, collaborative learning, peer tutoring, or scaffolding within the zone of proximal development (discussed in your child development text).

You may have noted that the younger "child-teacher" (aged 5–9) had more difficulty providing effective assistance or guidance than the older "child-teacher" or adult (e.g., see Rogoff, 1990; Siegler, 1998). Younger "child-teachers" may sometimes try to do too much (take over the task) or too little (insist that the learner do it without guidance), and may not provide hints and assistance that help the learner (do not match his or her level of understanding). However, even young children may provide appropriate assistance when they have expertise and extensive experience performing a task (some may have with constructing Lego models or playing computer games) and perceive the task as recreational (not an adult task) (e.g., Rogoff, 1998). Furthermore, when teachers encourage and support peer interaction in cooperative classroom learning (e.g., Damon, 1984; Slavin, 1997), children may learn to be helpful and develop skills in academic interactions.

One particular skill needed for successful academic and social interactions is the ability to see from the perspective of others; Strategy 4.3 allows for examining this critical cognitive ability in children.

———✦✦✦———

PERSPECTIVE-TAKING

For educators to help children develop competencies in a variety of areas (e.g., problem-solving, peer tutoring, reading comprehension), it is necessary to understand something about their developing perspective-taking abilities. To reveal potential age-related differences in children's perspective-taking abilities and understanding of others' intentions, the following strategy (Strategy 4.3) incorporates four classic tasks used by developmental researchers. The first task, an adaptation of Piaget and Inhelder's (1969) three-mountains task, involves asking children to take the visual perspective of another. The second task, an adaptation of Krauss and Glucksberg's (1969) phone task, requires children to accommodate another's perspective while giving explanations. The third and fourth tasks involve asking children to respond to hypothetical story dilemmas, such as those developed by Selman (1981) and Piaget (1932/1965). Children's abilities to interpret events from various perspectives and evaluate the intentions of others are examined in these tasks. Because researchers have found that children sometimes demonstrate advanced perspective-taking skills and moral reasoning when applying their thinking to real events in their everyday lives (e.g., Thorkildsen, 1989; Walker, Hennig, & Krettenauer, 2000), educators are also encouraged to create their own authentic tasks and stories/dilemmas for use here.

STRATEGY

4.3 *Perspective-Taking and Others' Intentions*

Ages 4–11

Participants: At least two children from each of the following age groups: (a) 4–5 years, (b) 6–7 years, (c) 8–9 years, (d) 10–11 years.

Materials:

Task 1: Stuffed animal, blocks or screens, small figures.

Task 2: Pretend phone (or walkie-talkie), board or screen, set of pictures with irregular designs.

Task 3: No materials necessary; may use drawing of kitten in tree.

Task 4: No materials necessary; may use drawings of activities.

Procedure:

Task 1: This task is appropriate to conduct with children from the first two age groups (see Figure 4.1). Set up small figures on various props (e.g., blocks) or

Figure 4.1

between screens so that some can be seen from the perspective of the stuffed animal sitting in one place but not from other places. Move the stuffed animal to various places or positions, and ask the child to tell you what the stuffed animal sees. Record the child's accurate and inaccurate responses.

Task 2: This task is appropriate for all of the age groups involved. Set up a screen or board between the two children and give each a "pretend phone" (or other such apparatus) to talk to one another. Give each child the same set of cards with irregular shapes (or other drawings that can be distinguished from one another may be described) and show them that the sets of cards are indeed identical before they begin. Then ask each child to choose one card at a time and explain the drawing on the card in enough detail so that the child on the other side of the screen/board can find the "correct" card. Repeat the procedure with each child in turn until most sets of the cards have been described. (For younger children, you may want to substitute three-dimensional forms or blocks for cards, and ask them to explain to their peer how to build what they are building.)

Task 3: Tell the story Holly and the kitten (you may substitute familiar characters and experiences).

> Holly is an 8–year-old girl who likes to climb trees. She is the best tree climber in the neighborhood. One day while climbing down from a tall tree, she falls, but does not hurt herself. Her father sees her fall. He is upset and asks her to promise not to climb trees anymore. Holly promises.
>
> Later that day, Holly and her friends meet Shawn. Shawn's kitten is caught in a tree and can't get down. Something has to be done right away or the kitten may fall. Holly is the only one who climbs trees well enough to reach the kitten and get it down but she remembers her promise to her father (Selman, 1976, p. 302).

Follow with interview questions similar to those Selman used: 1. Does Holly know how Shawn feels about the kitten? How does she know? 2. How will Holly's father feel if he finds out she climbed the tree? Why? 3. How does Holly think her father will feel if he finds out she climbed the tree? 4. What would you do if you were Holly?

Task 4: Tell a pair of stories about two characters-one causing considerable damage unintentionally, one causing negligible damage as a result of intentional wrongdoing. The following pair of stories are adapted from Piaget's (1965) work. (You may want to create similar stories.)

> A boy named Pete was called to come to dinner by his mom. He goes into the kitchen where his family usually eats. Behind the door to the kitchen was a box full of 12 glasses that his mom just bought. He couldn't have known that the box of glasses was there. He goes in, the door knocks against the box, and all 12 glasses get broken!
>
> A boy named Joe tried to get some cookies from on top of the refrigerator when his mother wasn't looking. He climbed up on a chair and tried to reach the cookies, but the cookie jar was too far back and he couldn't get to it and have any cookies. But while he was trying to get the cookies he knocked over a new glass. The glass fell down and broke.

Follow with questions such as the following: Are the two boys/girls equally guilty (wrong)? Or is one naughtier (more guilty) than the other? Why?

Recording and Interpreting Observations and Responses

Record children's responses and explanations and separate them by age group. Examine responses for age-related patterns. If your participants responded like many children in previous studies, the youngest children (4–5 years) responded quite differently than the older children. For example, the youngest children probably had more difficulty than older children (a) seeing objects from various positions (Task 1), (b) explaining cards adequately so that others could locate them (Task 2), (c) noting differences between Holly's, her father's, and Shawn's reactions based on their limited information (Task 3), and (d) considering characters' intentions in their judgments of "naughtiness" (Task 4). The largest discrepancies in responses were probably demonstrated between children 4–5- and 8–9 years old, corresponding with significant cognitive shifts in thinking occurring at about 6–7 years (see your child development text). In particular, cognitive development theorists, like Piaget and Selman, note advances in children's abilities to decenter from their own perspective, see events from two perspectives simultaneously, and distinguish one's perspective from others. Selman (1981) explains further advances in children's perspective-taking abilities occurring at about age 10 to 15. Thus, you may have noted that the oldest children interviewed were better able to consider how a third person might view an event (i.e., Holly's dilemma) from his or her perspective, as well as the parties involved (see your child development text for further explanation).

There is less consistency in researchers' findings and explanations regarding age differences in children's consideration of intention (Task 4). You may have found, like Piaget and other researchers, that only the older children consistently claimed the intentional misbehavior was naughtier. On the other hand, you may have noted that some of the younger children considered intention of the character in judging the morality of the behavior. Educators cannot assume that children's perspectives about such events are the same as adults; developmental psychologists propose that both children's social experiences and their developing cognitive abilities explain such differences. For example, experiences with close friends and parents may contribute to children's abilities to take others' perspectives and demonstrate sympathy (e.g., Eisenberg & Fabes, 1998).

————※※※————

CONSERVATION AND CLASSIFICATION

Children's abilities to conserve and classify influence their abilities to make sense of the social and physical world. In this section, interviewers are encouraged to conduct some conservation and problem-solving tasks to examine patterns in children's thinking. Strategy 4.4 allows educators to examine developmental changes in children's tendencies to conserve through use of Piaget's classic conservation tasks (refer to your child development text). The purpose of Strategy 4.5 is to reveal children's developing understandings of classes and relations.

STRATEGY

4.4   *Conservation Tasks*

Ages 5–9

Participants: Select at least two children from each of the following age groups: (a) 4–5 years, (b) 6–7 years, (c) 8–9 years.

Materials: 3 cups or glasses (see below); playdough or clay; 7 checker or candy pieces or pennies.

Procedure: Ask individual children to participate in the following tasks.

Conservation of Liquid. Place two glasses of identical shape and size filled with liquid, and a third empty glass of another size and shape (tall and thin, or short and wide). Ask about the filled glasses, "Is there just as much to drink in both glasses?" If the child questions whether they are equal, add or pour liquid until the child is convinced that there is an equal amount to drink, then ask the child, "If I pour one of these into this (third) glass, will there be just as much to drink in each glass?" (Point to the two glasses with liquid.) After the child makes a prediction, pour the contents of one of the glasses into the third glass *while the child observes,* and then ask, "Is there as much to drink in this glass as in the

---

Record Form 4.4: Conservation Tasks

	Prediction	Conclusion	Explanation	Conserver?
Child 1 Age ____				
Liquid				
Mass				
Number				
Child 2 Age ____				
Liquid				
Mass				
Number				

other one?" followed by the question, "Why is that?" Record the child's responses to all three questions (prediction, conclusion, explanation) in a chart like Record Form 4.4.

Conservation of Mass. To examine conservation of mass, use a similar procedure as for the conservation of liquid. Show two equal balls of playdough or clay and ask, "Do both balls have just as much clay/playdough?" Then ask, "Do I have as much if I roll one of the balls out like this (like a hotdog)?" Why?

Conservation of Number. Perform the same procedure as in the last two activities making two lines of candies, pennies, or other small pieces (checkers). Ask the child if there are as many objects (e.g., candies to eat) in both lines after spreading out one line. You may want to record child's responses in Record Form 4.4 and note whether or not their explanations demonstrate their ability to conserve.

Interpreting Responses and Observations

If the children involved in these tasks performed like many others, you noted differences between the youngest and oldest children's responses. Children who concluded that the amounts did not change despite the transformation and provided a logical explanation, are *conservers*. (Another clear sign that children are "true" conservers is if they look as if they would like to exclaim, "Well, duh," or question your intelligence for asking the question!) Children who concluded that one amount was more or less (with conviction) are *non-conservers*; it is likely that they explained the change in terms of its appearance (e.g., "it looks like more"). (See your child development text for other possible explanations.)

You also may have observed a child who does not show a clear preference for either conclusion. For example, a child may respond hesitantly or without conviction and appear to vacillate between concentrating on one or the other stimulus (e.g., the tall or wider glass); this child may be transitioning to a conserver perspective. In addition, you also may have interacted with a child who conserved in some tasks and not others; Piaget referred to this variability as *horizontal decalage*. Other cognitive theorists suggest that such inconsistent responding refutes Piaget's assumptions about general underlying cognitive structures and stages in general (see your child development text for a complete discussion).

According to Piaget and other researchers, the ability to conserve has important implications for children's understanding of aspects of the physical and social world. For example, conservation requires the ability to mentally reverse actions; this ability may assist in solving subtraction and other mathematical problems.

The following strategy (Strategy 4.5) incorporates the use of Piagetian-like class inclusion, multiple classification, and seriation tasks to examine elementary-age children's understanding of classes and relations (e.g., Ginsburg & Opper, 1988). In addition, a task designed to reveal advances in older children's and adolescents' awareness of interrelations and complex classification systems is suggested. Again, observers are encouraged to create their own authentic equivalents of such tasks (some ideas for adaptations are suggested).

STRATEGY

4.5   *Classes and Relations Tasks*

Ages 4–14

Participants: Select at least two children from each of the following age-groups: (a) 4–5 years, (b) 7–8 years, (c) 9–10 years, (Task 3 and 4 only) (d) 12–14 years (Task 4 only)

Materials:

Task 1: Superset of 10 objects (e.g., toy animals, flowers), with 1 subset of 7 of a kind (e.g., cats, daisies) and 1 subset of 3 of a kind (e.g., dogs, roses).

Task 2: 8 sticks (or straws) of various lengths.

Task 3: 3 × 3 matrix with stimuli that vary along two dimensions, such as shape (square, circle, triangle) and color (black, white, red); the last space in the matrix is left blank (see Figure 4.2). Four stimulus choices, including correct choice for the blank space. (A similar matrix can be set up using 3–dimensional materials, such as blocks.)

Task 4: Group of about 20 or more photos or pictures of people (e.g., students in a school yearbook) or objects (e.g., animals, dinosaurs) familiar to children.

Procedure: Perform each of the following tasks with children individually.

Task 1: Class Inclusion: Present the superset of objects (e.g., toy animals, flowers) to children (ages 4–8), and ask, "Are there more cats (daisies) or animals (flowers)?" Record their responses, and then ask them to explain their answers (i.e., "Why did you say _____.").

Task 2: Seriation: Present 7 sticks (or straws) in a random order to children (ages 4–8) and ask them to arrange the sticks or straws in order from shortest to longest (leave the eighth medium stick out). If children are able to accomplish this task, ask them to insert the new stick or straw of medium length in the right spot.

Figure 4.2

Observe whether children find the correct placement of the new stick, and describe their approach to solving the task (e.g., use of trial-and-error).

Task 3: Multiple Classification: Show children the matrix and direct their attention to the missing space by pointing. Tell them that one of the objects (show the four stimuli) belongs there, and ask them to choose the correct one and then explain their choice. Record each child's selection and explanation.

Task 4: Higher-Order Classes, Interrelations: Ask children to divide or sort the pictures of people or animals (or other familiar objects) into groups, and then explain their groupings (classes) (e.g., "Why did you put these people/animals together?"). Then ask them if there is any other way to put these people/animals together, and follow up with a similar question. Note the number and variety of ways that children show and explain relations among relations and about classes of classes (may be shown in a diagram constructed by you or the child).

Adaptations

The first three tasks can be adapted to increase the challenge level by simply adding more objects, sticks, or stimuli. For example, presenting a dozen sticks of various lengths would make the seriation task more complex, and showing a 4 × 4 matrix would make the multiple-classification task more complex.

There are nearly limitless ways for adapting the tasks to make them interesting and relevant for children. For example, the seriation task (Task 2) can be modified in a fun way by asking children to put their classmates in order from shortest to tallest. A classification task (Task 4) can be developed by asking children to create a family tree to show the interrelationships among members across generations; interviewers/observers could note age-related differences in children's abilities to comprehend the classification system (e.g., understand that one's grandfather can be another's uncle). In addition, all tasks can be modified by substituting objects or stimuli familiar to children. For example, one could take advantage of elementary children's passions for collecting and classifying Pokemon cards as a rich opportunity for examining their understanding of classes and relations (however, it is likely that adults would need older child "experts" to act as interpreters).

Interpreting Responses and Observations

It is likely that differences in children's responses to these tasks were observed, particularly between the 4–5–year-olds and older children. Regarding the class inclusion task (Task 1), it is likely that the youngest children responded that there were more objects in the subset (e.g., cats, daisies) than in the superset (e.g., animals, flowers), and older children correctly identified the superset as having more. Piaget and others interpret the younger children's responses as stemming from their preoperational tendencies to focus on a single dimension or aspect of a problem, explained by their difficulty with keeping more than one aspect of a problem in mind simultaneously (i.e., an individual cat belongs to both a subset of cats and to a superset of animals). A similar explanation is offered for the youngest children's difficulty with the seriation and other classification tasks. For example, 4–5–year-old children may have been able to correctly order the lengths of the original set of sticks (Task 2), but had difficulty placing the new stick without extensive use of trial-and-error. Again, it is hypothesized that preoperational children have difficulty simultaneously viewing the new stick as both smaller than one stick and larger than another similar in size. Likewise, in response to the matrix task (Task 3), the youngest children were likely to have chosen an object that contains one of the desired attributes or dimensions (shape or color), but not both to complete the matrix correctly. In contrast, all of the 9–10–year-olds and most of the 7–8–year-olds probably chose the correct object coordinating both attributes (shape and color), demonstrating their concrete operational ability to consider classes and relations together (e.g., Ginsburg & Opper, 1988; Siegler, 1998).

With regard to the last classification task, you were likely to see the most complex classification systems and explanations displayed by the oldest age groups. In particular, you may have noted pre- or early adolescents' abilities to construct or diagram a number of classes (e.g., types of students, such as preppies, jocks; types of dinosaurs), and higher order classes of the groups (i.e., those who do well in school vs. not; carnivores vs. vegetarians), using a systematic approach. Formal operational reasoning may enable adolescents to think systematically about relations among relations and about classes of classes, or reason about interrelations and classification systems (refer to your child development text). On the other hand, you may have observed that younger children with extensive knowledge and experience with the objects to be classified are able to develop complex classification systems similar to those constructed by older children (e.g., Case, 1998).

Children's classification skills are also interesting to observe as they are developed in joint activity with skilled partners (see your child development text for studies on guided participation). For example, Rogoff and her colleagues (1994) observed mothers assisting their elementary-age children with home-like (i.e., food sorting) and school-like (i.e., photo sorting) classification tasks. In particular, one can observe the sensitivity of the instructional supports provided and how children gradually become better able to manage classification tasks.

———※※———

SCIENTIFIC AND MATHEMATICAL THINKING

Children's abilities to solve problems and systematically test solutions develop with age and experience. In the next strategy (Strategy 4.6), interviewers are introduced to a familiar game that may be used to reveal children's abilities to plan and test hypotheses to derive solutions. It is a modification of the popular "twenty questions" game, as adapted by Bruner (1966). Child study students are encouraged to create their own version of this game as an alternative strategy.

STRATEGY

Hypothesis Testing: Twenty Questions Game

Ages 7–14

Participants: Select at least two children from each of the following age groups: (a) 7–9 years, (b) 10–12 years, (c) 13–14 years

Materials: Deck of playing cards (42 cards)

Procedure: Show the child the set of 42 cards displayed in six rows of seven cards each. Ask the child to determine which card you are thinking of (which is correct). Explain that she or he is only allowed to ask questions to which you can answer yes or no. The object of the game is to find the correct card with asking as few questions as possible. Record the child's questions.

Interpretation Responses and Observations

Adolescents are expected to demonstrate more elegant planning than children (Siegler, 1998). They are more likely to formulate and systematically test hypotheses to narrow the options. For example, the most efficient plan is to use a "halving" strategy (e.g., "is it in the top half"); this strategy allows the child to find the correct solution in seven questions or less. Other strategies may be less efficient, but still allow the child to rule out several possibilities at a time with each question. This ability to systematically plan and test hypotheses is considered by some, notably Piaget, to be an aspect of formal operational thinking most likely developed in adolescence (see your child development text). (However, Siegler [1998] and others have pointed out that scientific reasoning continues to remain a challenge throughout adulthood.) Children, in contrast, are more likely to use trial-and-error strategies, and may pursue questions that test some of the same possibilities that previous questions should have eliminated. For example, they may have eliminated an area, but ask whether the card is in a row within that area later. Children's propensity to use trial-and-error strategies deserves consideration when planning instructional activities.

In the next strategy (Strategy 4.7), observers are encouraged to look carefully at children's use of addition strategies. This strategy is based for the most part on Siegler's (1996, 1998) research and descriptions of ways that children solve addition and other problems. Rather than looking for consistencies in the ways that children solve problems at different points in development (as in the previous strategies), this strategy allows educators to examine diverse ways that children approach problems.

———

STRATEGY

4.7 | *Arithmetic Strategies*

Ages 4–10

Participants: Select at least two children from each of the following grade levels: (a) pre-K, (b) grades 1–2, (c) grades 3–5

Materials: Pencil and paper, counting pieces (optional), stopwatch

Procedure: Ask children to solve five single-digit addition problems any way that they want (limit to addends of 5 for the pre-K children e.g., 4+2, 5+1). (You may find it appropriate to present the problems in writing for older children, and verbally for younger children; ask children for their preferences.) If it is not apparent

Record Form 4.7: Arithmetic Strategies Chart

	Guess	Show	Count from 1	Min	Decompose	Retrieve	Other
Pre-K							
Child 1							
Child 2							
Grades 1–2							
Child 1							
Child 2...							
Grade 3 and on							
Child 1							
Child 2...							

ask them to explain or show you how they solved the problems. Observe the type and frequency of strategies used (listed below); also note the speed and accuracy of children's responses.

Addition Strategies

Guessing (low accuracy and no overt strategy use).

Counting fingers or objects (starting from 1).

Showing fingers (demonstrating answer without counting them).

Retrieval (answering without showing overt behavior or strategy use).

Min strategy (counting from the larger addend, e.g., to solve 6 + 4, start with 6 and count 7, 8, 9, 10, so answer is 10).

Decomposition (dividing a problem into two simpler ones, as in adding 9 + 4 by thinking 10 + 4 is 14, 9 is one less than 10, so 9 + 4 is 13)

Recording Responses

Use a chart like the one depicted above to record the number of times (out of five) that each child used a particular strategy. Write beside the number the *approximate* time (in seconds/minutes) it took the child to respond. Note also if the child was inaccurate.

Follow-Up Questions

To find out about the range of strategies available to individual children, you may want to question child participants who appeared to use just one strategy about other ways to solve the problem (e.g., "How would you explain to a younger child how to add? If she or he didn't like that way, can you think of another way to do it?") (questions adapted from Siegler, 1996). (Young children may have trouble expressing their thoughts in words.) Note the diverse strategies available for use by individuals.

Interpreting Responses and Observations

You may have noticed some developmental trends in the use of strategies. For example, one would expect that children would make more use of retrieval and decomposition strategies and less use of guessing and counting from one as they progress through the primary grades; the use of min strategies appears to reach a peak in first grade (see Siegler, 1996 for a review). (Curiously, neither teachers nor parents usually teach the min strategy; children appear to discover it with experience solving addition problems.) One also would expect that with age children will increase in their speed and accuracy rates in solving addition problems. Although by third grade children retrieve most answers to addition problems, at no age do most people consistently retrieve all answers to single-digit addition problems; thus you may have noted some use of less efficient strategies even in your oldest age group. Nonetheless, with development, children increasingly use more efficient strategies to solve problems.

From an educator's perspective, what may be most compelling about these observations is that individual children are aware of and utilize a variety of strategies to solve problems. Some teachers are taking advantage of children's use of diverse strategies to help them engage in stimulating conversations about each others' mathematical problem-solving approaches (e.g., see Wood, Cobb, & Yackel, 1992).

———✻✻✻———

LANGUAGE AND LITERACY

Although children come to school with fairly sophisticated language skills, they continue to develop appreciation of and abilities to reflect on the value of written language and the use of spoken language throughout their school years. In this section, strategies for examining children's purposes and strategies for reading are recommended. In addition, strategies for tapping children's uses and understandings of complex language in literature, media, and everyday conversations are introduced.

STRATEGY

4.8 Reading Strategies and Purposes

Ages 5–14

Participants: Select at least two children from each of the following grade levels: (a) kindergarten, (b) grades 1–2, (c) grades 3–4, (d) grades 5–8

Materials: Variety of reading materials, including some appropriate for children in elementary and middle grades: e.g., picture and story books, magazines, newspapers, TV guide, phone book.

Procedure:

Part 1: First, ask children about the purposes of various reading materials presented (e.g., "Why do people read _____?"). Then ask about the materials that *they* read, how often they read, and for what purpose. For example, you may create interview questions such as the following:

1. Tell me about the kinds of reading that *you* do (show the various reading materials). What kinds of reading do you like? Why? When and where do you read? With whom?

2. What kinds of reading do you do *just for fun* (not because you have to in school)? About how much time do you spend reading *just because you want to* each day? Each week? (Note that the youngest children will probably have trouble answering this general question. Instead, you may want to ask specific questions, such as, "Do you choose to read sometimes at school when you don't have to? When do you get to read at home? (After school? Before you go to bed?)"

Part 2: Ask children to choose something from among the materials provided to read to you for a few minutes. You may want to ask some follow-up questions to elicit their understanding of the text, how they came to that understanding, and what they would do if they didn't understand (again, young children may have difficulty responding to these questions). Take note of reading strategies and skills that may be demonstrated during this activity, such as

Visual cue recognition (use signs or pictures to recognize words).

Phonetic cue recognition ("sounding out" words).

Automatic word recognition (retrieve individual words efficiently).

Fluency (smooth reading).

Strategic reading (reading to obtain new information, alter strategies appropriately, e.g., Skim to find a fact, read slowly and carefully for understanding).

Corrective strategies (e.g., re-reading, reading ahead to resolve an inconsistency, looking up or asking about an unfamiliar word).

You may want to record your notes and interpretations in a chart like Record Form 4.8.

Interpreting Responses and Observations

You may have noted from your summary of children's responses to questions in Part 1 that even the youngest children could explain the appropriate uses of reading materials (e.g., Weiss & Hagan, 1988). Understanding the function of reading in everyday life is important for the development of literacy. You also may have noted some age-related differences in how much time children reported reading for fun (leisure reading). Unfortunately, although adolescents become more proficient readers, research shows that they report enjoying reading less (e.g., Wigfield et al., 1991). They may also spend less time in daily leisure reading than do younger children, important because reading achievement is related to time spent reading on a daily basis (National Assessment of Educational Progress, 1998). Educators who are aware of such potential declines can take steps to foster engagement in reading.

It is likely that you observed evidence of older children's increasing reading proficiencies. For example, kindergartners likely revealed abilities to "read" a few words on signs or pictures using visual cues; first and second graders likely demonstrated abilities to sound out words; and third graders probably retrieved many words easily, enabling them to read quite fluently (e.g., Spear-Swerling & Sternberg, 1994). You may

Record Form 4.8 (Part 2): Reading Skills and Strategies

	Visual Cues	Phonetic Cues	Automaticity	Fluency	Strategies (describe)	Other
Kindergarten						
Child 1						
Child 2...						
Grades 1–2						
Child 1						
Child 2...						
Grades 3–4						
Child 1						
Child 2...						
Grades 5–8						
Child 1						
Child 2...						

have observed how older children (ages 10 and above) used different strategies for different reading purposes (e.g., finding facts, understanding meaning). The conscious use of flexible strategies is expected to help children read more effectively (e.g., Santrock, 1998, Siegler, 1998). This is seen, for example, in **reciprocal teaching** methods, in which elementary children are taught to strategically monitor their comprehension of reading materials (e.g., Brown, 1994) (refer to your child development text).

Of course, you also may have noted some individual differences in approaches to reading not related to age or grade level. One would expect differences among children's leisure and strategic reading related to their opportunities and experiences in the family (e.g., availability of reading materials, languages spoken) as well as in the classroom (e.g., reading programs).

As children develop logical and abstract thought, they use and understand language differently and attend to different aspects of literature and media. For example, they become better conversationalists and better able to understand abstract language, such as satire and metaphor (e.g., Demorest et al., 1984). Satire refers to the use of irony or humor to expose absurdity. Satire may be seen in older children and adolescents' labels or nicknames for others. It also is seen in their selected reading materials and other media. For example, satire is found in cartoons or comic strips in children's magazines, such as *Sports Illustrated for Kids*, and in books, such as J.K. Rowling's popular *Harry Potter* series. Metaphor is defined as an implied comparison between two ideas that is conveyed by the abstract meaning contained in the words. Understanding of metaphors is often examined in questions such as, "How is a _____ like a _____?" Children's understanding of such abstract use of language influences their abilities to understand literature and media as well as everyday conversations.

———※———

In the next strategy (Strategy 4.9), guidelines for observing abstract language use and understanding in everyday life as well as in structured activities are suggested. It may be helpful to review the language development chapter (in the primary text) and spend some time informally observing children's natural language use (e.g., on the playground) before conducting these observations (see Chapter 2). Student observers will need to first conduct a search for (G-rated) cartoons or comics in newspapers or magazines or excerpts from books to show children and young adolescents; this first step might be best accomplished working in collaboration with a group from class.

STRATEGY

4.9 Use of Language: Conversations, Metaphor, and Satire

Ages 7–14

Participants: At least two children from each of the following age groups: (a) 7–9 years, (b) 10–12 years, (c) 13–14 years.

Materials: Cartoons or magazines depicting satire; list of possible metaphorical comparisons

Procedure:

Anecdotes: Everyday Conversations (see Chapter 2). Observe natural conversations of children on the playground, in the lunchroom, or in another informal conversational setting. Write excerpts of conversations that include use of nicknames (satire), jokes, and storytelling. Note children's abilities to converse with others (e.g., take turns speaking and listening, consider the perspective and interest of the listener).

Task 1: Show children cartoons or other reading material involving satire. Note children's laughter and other emotional expressions, and ask them what they thought was funny and why.

Task 2: Present a list of possible metaphorical comparisons ("How is a ___ like a ___?") Ask children to give as many ideas as they can.

Interpreting Responses and Observations

It is likely that you observed some rather dramatic differences between the oldest and youngest children's conversations. Young adolescents are expected to demonstrate better skills in joke-telling, storytelling, and conversing in general with others (e.g., Santrock, 2001, 8/e). They also are expected to better understand satire and metaphor depicted in media as well as everyday conversations. Thus, you may have noticed that older children and adolescents found ironic segments of reading materials funny and interesting and were better able to explain how to "get it" than younger children. Such understandings are important for engaging children in literature.

—— ‡‡‡ ——

PLANNING AND MONITORING

Children's developing abilities to self-monitor and plan may help explain what and how much they study. Educators may use the next strategy (Strategy 4.10) to examine children's understanding of their memory processes and the following strategy (Strategy 4.11) to examine their abilities to plan and solve problems in advance. The tasks are similar to those used by a variety of researchers (e.g., Cultice, Somerville, & Wellman, 1983; Flarell, Friedrichs & Hoyt, 1970; Kreutzen, Leonard, & Flarell, 1975; Schneider & Pressley, 1997). It is important to use caution when evaluating young children's understandings of their mental processes; young children's verbal skills may be inadequate to express their understandings. Nonetheless, the following strategies may be helpful in revealing some common age-related changes in children's memory awareness and planning that influence their ways of studying in school.

STRATEGY

4.10   *Memory Awareness and Self-Monitoring*

Ages 4–13

Participants: At least two children from each of the following age groups: (a) 4–6 years, (b) 7–9 years, (c) 10–13 years.

Materials: Set of 10 pictures; short story or poem; school yearbook (or variety of class photos).

Procedure:

Task 1: Show children a set of ten pictures. Ask them (1) "Tell me how many pictures you think you can remember if you looked at them for just a minute?" Then ask, (2) "What is the best way for you to remember (memorize) all these pictures? and follow with (3) "Would it be easier for you to *tell me* (recall) all the pictures you have seen or *point to* (recognize) the pictures you have seen if I showed them to you?" Record the children's predictions and strategy choices. Next, ask the children to study the pictures for a minute or two, then "hide" the pictures and ask them to tell you all the pictures that they can remember.

Task 2: Show children an age-appropriate short story or poem, and ask them, (4) "Would it be easier to remember the *whole* story/poem or just what it is *about?*" (5) "If I asked you to tell me this story/poem, how would you try to remember it?" Prompts: "What would you do? Think about?" Record the children's responses.

Task 3: Show children photographs of students that they know to varying degrees (e.g., from a school yearbook, or variety of class portraits). Ask them to (6) "Tell me (or point to) who you know and don't know by name." Then point out some students that they did not know and ask them (7) "Would you remember this girl/boy's name if I told you the names of all the students in this class?" Follow up by asking for the names of some "forgotten" students, and check to see if children correctly identified students that they expected to recall if given a class list of names. Record children's predictions for recall, and the accuracy of their predictions (whether they could remember the name with clues).

Adaptation

The first task can be adapted by placing ten different objects on a tray, and asking children to tell you how many they can remember if they only see them for a few seconds; this kind of memory game is frequently played at children's parties.

Interpreting Responses and Observations

If the children you interviewed are similar to children in previous studies, the older children were more likely to recognize the fallibility of memory (see review of such research in Siegler, 1998 and your child development text). For example, you may have found that the youngest children expected to remember more pictures (Task 1), but actually remembered fewer. You also may have noted that more of the older children replied that recognition is easier than recall, and that remembering the content of a story/poem is easier than remembering it verbatim. In addition you may have noted that although young children were overly optimistic about their abilities to remember in some cases, they may have been fairly accurate in predicting who (of the children in school) they could recognize with clues.

Children's abilities to recognize the limitations of their memories influence how they study. Fortunately, research indicates that grade school children can be trained to monitor their memories, and such training has positive effects on their use of study strategies (e.g., Schneider & Bjorklund, 1998). Children also can be assisted with making efficient study plans.

The next strategy is an adaptation of route planning tasks used to examine children's tendencies to plan in advance of solving problems (Gardner & Rogoff, 1990). This strategy involves asking children to devise efficient routes through a maze. Educators may adapt this strategy using authentic tasks, such as asking children to plan how to get to a certain location avoiding wrong turns (e.g., use a map to plan a field-trip), or how to obtain items on a grocery list without backtracking. (e.g., Gauvain & Rogoff, 1989; Hudson, Shapiro, & Sosa, 1995).

STRATEGY

4.11 *Planning and Problem-Solving*

Ages 4–14

Participants: Select at least two children from each of the following age groups: (a) 4–6 years, (b) 7–10 years, (c) 11–14 years.

Materials: Age-appropriate mazes (may be created or purchased at most discount stores).

Procedures:

Step 1: Check the child's skill at completing mazes by having him or her attempt some samples. Choose an appropriately challenging maze for the child (i.e., takes a few minutes to complete).

Step 2: Tell the child that you have a maze to complete, and the object of the game is to arrive at the end of the maze *avoiding wrong turns*. Tell the child that you will give him or her time to think about what to do, and to tell you when he or she is ready. Observe the child's planning behavior during the waiting time, and note the approximate amount of time the child chose to plan.

Step 3: When the child is ready, ask what she or he thought about before trying the maze, and record explanations (young children may have difficulty with this request).

Step 4: Ask the child to complete the maze. Note the child's behavior, spontaneous comments, emotional expressions, and performance on the maze (e.g., the number of wrong turns made). You may want to record your observations of each child in a form like the following:

Record Form 4.11: Planning and Problem Solving

Age _____

Planning (before task)

    Time spent _____

    Child's behavior _____

    Child's explanation _____

Performance (during task)

    # of mistakes/wrong turns _____

    # of corrections _____

    Child's behavior/affect/spontaneous comments

Evaluation: Partial or elaborate planning

Interpreting Responses and Observations

Examine children's route-planning and performance on mazes across age groups. You likely observed differences in the extent of planning and the number of mistakes between the first two age groups. Previous research indicates that although children of all ages are responsive to task demands, older children are more likely to use strategies fitting the goals of the task than are younger children (e.g., Siegler, 1998). When instructed to attend to *accuracy* (as in this case), research shows that younger children (ages 4–7) tend to make partial plans (plan some of the route), proceed on mazes, and then correct their mistakes; in contrast, older children (ages 7–10) make elaborate plans (plan entire sequence) and fewer mistakes as a result (Gardner & Rogoff, 1990). However, if older children are instructed to attend to *speed*, they also make partial plans before proceeding with the task. Children's planning skills are important to consider when providing task instructions.

––––— ‡‡‡ ——––

ACTIVITY SETTINGS FOR TEACHING AND LEARNING

The strategy described in this section allows educators to observe activity settings that may provide more or less support for children's learning and development. Activity settings are defined as "contexts in which collaborative interaction, intersubjectivity, and assisted performance in *teaching* occurs..." (Tharp & Gallimore, 1988, p. 72). According to Tharp and Gallimore (1988, 1990) and other neo-Vygotskian theorists, **activity settings** must be created in schools to maximize opportunities for teachers and capable peers to assist children's learning (i.e., through scaffolding and other means of assistance) (see Strategy 4.2). In Strategy 4.12, observers are asked to follow children throughout their morning or afternoon in classrooms to examine their participation in various activity settings. In particular, the strategy calls for describing components of classroom activity settings as presented by Tharp and Gallimore.

STRATEGY

Instructional Interactions with Teachers and Students

Grades K-8

Participants: Select a child from each of the following grade levels: (a) K-2, (b) 3–5, (c) 6–8.

Materials: Clipboard and response charts (extras may be needed for frequent activity changes), watch.

Procedure: Choose a two-hour period during the morning or afternoon school day to observe; talk with teachers in advance to determine the best times to observe students in academic learning activities. Briefly describe learning activities that chil-

Record Form 4.12: Activity Setting Descriptions

Grade _____   Time Observed: Morning   Afternoon

Brief description of child and major activities involved in during observation period.

_____

_____

_____

	Small Group with Teacher	Small Group with Peers	Independent Centers	Whole Group	Seatwork Self	Other: Mentor or Tutor
Who?						
What?						
When?						
# Minutes						
Where?						
Why?						
Child's Participation Rating (1–5)						

dren participate in throughout the time period, noting how long each separate activity lasts (describe nonacademic activities in the "other" category). Record Form 4.12 shows some common activity settings in elementary and middle schools: small group instructional activity with teacher, small group activity with peers, independent centers (work with materials mostly on own), whole group activity (teacher instructs large group of students), and seatwork (students work individually at their seats). Other types of learning activities may be added, such as individual work with the teacher, peer mentor, or tutor. For each separate activity setting, describe *who* is involved and how they were selected (e.g., talented readers), *when* the activity is scheduled and for how long, *where* the activity occurs, *what* the essential features of the activity are (including the actions of the teacher and student), and *why* the activity occurs (the major purpose of the activity and/or its product). Estimate target children's participation level by assigning a 1–5 rating (1= not participating, 5 = fully participating).

Adaptation

Observers may want to focus on the activities of a sample of children *within* rather than *across* grade levels. This observation may be valuable for identifying instructional opportunities for children with particular needs, strengths, and interests.

Interpreting Responses and Observations

Write a brief description of the major activity settings involving the target children (who, what, when, where, why). Evaluate children's opportunities for instructional assistance and guidance in each major activity setting as well as throughout the period of observation (see your child development text for discussion about providing assistance through the zone of proximal development). You may have sadly discovered, as did others (i.e., Tharp & Gallimore, 1988, 1990), that there were few opportunities in school for instructional interactions, conversation, and joint activity among teachers and children. On the other hand, you may have described some rich activity settings fostering teaching and learning opportunities. It may be worthwhile to share and discuss your observations and analysis with fellow students (omitting identifying information about individuals and schools).

———※※———

CONCEPTIONS OF INTELLIGENCE

The final strategy in this chapter provides sample interview questions for probing teachers' views of intelligence (see Chapter 2 for discussion of semi-structured interviews). The purpose of this strategy is to reveal important beliefs concerning student abilities that may have important implications for educational practice (e.g., Richardson, 1996). For example, teachers may endorse the concept of multiple intelligences mirroring contemporary psychologists' views such as those of Howard Gardner's (1993) or Robert Sternberg's (1985), or they may endorse a general concept of intelligence, and plan instructional activities in accordance with such views (see your child development text for a discussion).

STRATEGY

Interview with a Teacher: Views of Intelligence

Participants: A classroom teacher

Procedure: Ask a teacher if you could take about 10–15 minutes of his or her time to ask some questions about views of intelligence.

Sample Interview Questions:

1. How do you define intelligence? Or intelligences? (Do you accept a particular theorist's conception of intelligence, e.g., Howard Gardners?)

2. What are characteristics of intelligent behavior? (What are some examples of how students demonstrate intelligence?)

3. What can teachers or schools do to foster students' intellectual development? What are limitations or barriers to fostering intelligence?

4. How do your views of intelligence affect your classroom practices? (What are some examples?)

Adaptation: Interview with a Parent

Interview questions may be adapted as appropriate for parents (substituting "children" for "students"). Question 4 should refer to effects on parenting rather than classroom practices.

Interpreting Responses and Observations

Preserving exact words whenever possible, record the teacher's responses. Then, prepare an analysis of the responses by making connections between views and descriptions of intelligence expressed by teachers and those described by theorists and others (see your child development text). For example, you may note that teachers refer to single or multiple intelligences of students and adapt instructional practices accordingly (e.g., through assignment of roles or projects to individuals). Teachers also may demonstrate beliefs consistent with an incremental (malleable) or entity (fixed) view of intelligence (e.g., Dweck, 1999). On the other hand, you may note that teachers have personal views of intelligence, not easily connected to a particular theory or practice. You may want to hypothesize about how such views affect instructional practices, interactions with children, and children's learning and motivation (see next chapter).

———‡‡‡———

CHAPTER SUMMARY

Through chapter observations and interviews, educators are expected to further their understandings of the ways in which children develop, learn, and make sense of the world in school settings. Educators are expected to develop skills of "seeing" evidence of children's thinking and learning revealed in behavior in light of contemporary theoretical perspectives and research (described in child development texts). Furthermore, educators are expected to gather ideas for creating developmentally-appropriate instructional practices and settings to foster children's learning and development in school.

REFLECTION QUESTIONS

1. How might educators incorporate constructive play activities in their classrooms to foster children's cognitive development? (Strategies 4.1, 4.2)

2. How might different cognitive theorists, such as Vygotsky and Piaget, explain the meaning of some of the play interactions you observed? (Strategies 4.1, 4.2)

3. How could children's perspective-taking abilities influence their collaboration with peers on academic tasks? (Strategies 4.2, 4.3)

4. How could children's responses to conservation or classification tasks be explained by cognitive theorists other than Piaget? (Strategies 4.4, 4.5)

5. How are children's conservation and classification skills reflected in their academic activities? (Strategies 4.4, 4.5)

6. How can educators foster children's abilities to generate efficient and diverse plans and problem-solving strategies? (Strategies 4.6, 4.7, 4.11)

7. How can teachers take advantage of children's informal literacy-related experiences to enhance academic instruction? (Strategies 4.8, 4.9)

8. How could children's memory awareness or approaches to problem-solving (planning) affect their study skills and habits? (Strategies 4.10, 4.11)

9. How could the creation of different activity settings enhance opportunities for providing assistance in the zone of proximal development (ZPD)? Provide examples of different settings. (Strategy 4.12)

10. How might educators' conceptions of intelligence affect their interactions with students, instruction, and evaluation practices? (Strategy 4.13)

RESOURCES

Duckworth, E. (1996). *The having of wonderful ideas and other essays on teaching and learning*. New York: Teachers College Press.

Forman, G., & Kuschner, D. (1983). *Piaget for teaching children: The child's construction of knowledge*. Washington DC: National Association for the Education of Young Children.

Rogoff, B. (Ed.) (2001). *Learning together: Children and adults in a school community*. New York: Oxford University Press.

Siegler, R. (1998). *Children's thinking*. Third Edition. Upper Saddle River, NJ: Prentice Hall.

Tharp, R., & Gallimore, R. (1988). *Rousing minds to life: Teaching, learning, and schooling in social context*. Cambridge: Cambridge University Press.

TIPS FOR TEACHERS

Classroom teachers may want to conduct periodic observations of their students' thinking, task approaches, and skills revealed in informal school activities by adapting Strategies 4.1, 4.2, or 4.9. Maintaining and reviewing anecdotal records of such observations may provide teachers with an expanded view of their students' abilities and interests, as well as offer ideas for instruction and grouping of students. In addition to these strategies, Strategy 4.3 (Task 3) can also be modified for the purpose of identifying peer tutors and roles for students in collaborative learning groups.

Tasks and games, such as those described in Strategies 4.4, 4.5, 4.6, and 4.11, can be incorporated as appropriate within academic instructional activities. Teachers may use these activities as a means for looking closely at the workings of their students' minds, and thus enhancing their chances for meeting those minds (develop intersubjectivity) (see Chapter 1). Olson and Bruner (1996) propose that "the first step in 'equipping' teachers (or parents) for their task is to provide them access to the best available understanding of the mind of the child" (p. 12–13). Teachers may be able to better assist child with reflecting on, monitoring, and directing their own thinking by making use of adapted Strategies 4.7, 4.8 (part 2), and 4.10.

For professional development purposes, teachers may want to reflect on and monitor their owns views of students' intelligences or abilities (Strategy 4.13), and how their views may be affecting their practices and interactions (e.g., assignment of challenging tasks and roles, praise for effort versus ability). They may question whether they are acting in ways to foster the development of each student's abilities. Teachers may also call for a colleague or mentor to help them carefully examine the purposes and uses of current activity settings in their classroom (Strategy 4.12). They can consider ways to create new settings to maximize opportunities for guided participation, and instructional activities and conversations. Periodic reflection on one's own thinking and instructional practice is considered essential for implementing "contemporary psychological perspectives" and social-constructivist educational practices to enhance children's learning and development (e.g., Anderson, et. al, 1995; Richardson, 1996).

REFERENCES

Anderson, L., Blumenfeld, P., Pintrich, P., Clark, D., Marx, R., and Peterson, P. (1995). Educational psychology for teachers: Reforming our courses, rethinking our roles. *Educational*

Psychologist, 30, 143–157.

Brown, A. (1994). The advancement of learning. *Educational Researcher, 23,* 4–12.

Bruner, J. (1966). *Toward a theory of instruction.* Cambridge, MA: Harvard University Press.

Case, R. (1998). The development of conceptual structures. In W. Damon (Series Ed.) and D. Kuhn and R. Siegler (Vol. Ed.), *Handbook of Child Psychology: Vol 2. Cognition, Perceptions, and Language* (pp. 745–800). New York: John Wiley.

Cultice, J., Somerville, S., and Wellman, H. (1983). Preschooler's memory monitoring: Feeling of knowing judgments. *Child Development, 54,* 1480–86.

Damon, W. (1984). Peer education: The untapped potential. *Journal of Applied Developmental Psychology, 5,* 331–343.

Demorest, A., Meyer, C., Phelps, E., Gardner, Hr., and Winner, E. (1984). Words speak louder than actions: Understanding deliberately false remarks. *Child Development, 55,* 1527–1534.

Dweck, C. (1999). *Self-theories: Their role in motivation, personality and development.* Ann Arbor, MI: Psychology Press.

Eisenberg, N., and Fabes (1998). Prosocial development. In W. Damon (Series Ed.) and N. Eisenberg (Vol. Ed.), *Handbook of Child Psychology: Vol 3. Social, Emotional, and Personality Development* (pp. 701–778). New York: John Wiley.

Flavell, J., Green, F., and Flavell, E. (1970). Developmental changes in memorization processes. *Cognitive Psychology, 1,* 324–40.

Gallimore, R., and Tharp, R. (1990). Teaching mind in society. In L Moll (Ed.) *Vygotsky and education : Instructional implications and applications of sociohistorical psychology* (pp. 175–205).

Gardner, H. (1993). *Multiple intelligences: The theory in practice.* New York: Basic Books.

Gardner, W. and Rogoff, B. (1990). Children's deliberateness of planning according to task circumstances. *Developmental Psychology, 26,* 480–487.

Gauvain, M., and Rogoff, B. (1989). Collaborative problem-solving and children's planning skills. *Developmental Psychology 25,* 139–151.

Ginsburg, H., and Opper, S. (1988). *Piaget's theory of intellectual development,* 3rd ed. Englewood Cliffs, NJ: Prentice Hall.

Hudson, J., Shapiro, L., and Susa, B. (1995). Planning in the real world: Preschool children's scripts and plans for familiar events. *Child Development, 66,* 984–998.

Krauss, R., and Gluchkberg, S. (1969). The development of communication: Competence as a function of age. *Child development, 40,* 255–266.

Kreutzer, M., Leonard, C., and Flavell, J. (1975). An interview study of children's knowledge about memory. *Monographs of the Society for Research in Child Development, 40.*

National Assessment of Educational Progress (1998). The NAEP 1998 Reading Report Card: National and State Highlights. (nces.edu.gov.nationsreportcard).

Olson, D., and Bruner, J. (1996). Folk psycology and fok pedagogy. In D. Olson and N. Torrance (Eds.) *The Handbook of Education and Development: New Models of Learning, Teaching, and Schooling* (pp. 9–27). Malden, MA: Blackwell.

Piaget, J. (1932/1965). *The moral judgment of the child.* New York: Harcourt Brace Jovanovich.

Piaget, J. (1926). *The language and thought of the child.* New York: Norton.

Piaget, J., and Inhelder, B. (1969). *The psychology of the child.* London: Routledge & Kegan Paul.

Richardson, V. (1996). The role of attitudes and belief in learning to teach. In J. Sikula, T. Buttery, E. Guyton (Eds.) *Handbook of Research on Teacher Education* (2nd ed., pp. 1020119). New York: Prentice Hall.

Rogoff, B. (1990). *Apprenticeship in thinking: Cognitive development in social context.* New York: Oxford University Press.

Rogoff, B. (1998). Cognition as a collaborative process. In W. Damon (Series Ed.) and D. Kuhn and R. Siegler (Vol. Ed.), *Handbook of Child Psychology: Vol 2. Cognition, Perceptions, and Language* (pp. 679–744). New York: John Wiley.

Rogoff, B., and Lave, J. (1984). *Everyday cognition: Its development in social context.* Cambridge, MA: Harvard University Press.

Santrock, J. (2001). *Adolescence,* Ninth Edition. Boston, MA: McGraw-Hill.

Santrock, J. (2001). *Child development,* Eighth Edition. Boston, MA: McGraw-Hill.

Schneider, W., and Bjorklund, D. (1998). Memory. In W. Damon (Series Ed.) and D. Kuhn and R. Siegler (Vol. Ed.), *Handbook of Child Psychology: Vol 2. Cognition, Perceptions, and Language* (pp. 467–522). New York: John Wiley.

Selman, R. (1976). Social-cognitive understanding. In T. Likona (Ed.), *Moral development and behavior*. New York, Rinehart & Winston.

Selman, R. (1981). *The growth of interpersonal understanding*. New York: Academic Press.

Siegler, R. (1996). *Emerging minds: The process of thinking in children's thinking*. New York: Oxford University Press.

Siegler, R. (1998). *Children's thinking*. Third Edition. Upper Saddle River, NJ: Prentice-Hall.

Slavin, R. (1994). *Cooperative learning: Theory, Research, and Practice* (2nd edition). Boston: Allyn & Bacon.

Sneider, W. and Pressley, M. (1997). *Memory development between 2 and 20,* 2nd Edition. Mahmah, NJ: Erlbaum.

Spear-Swerling, L., and Sternberg, R. (1994). The road not taken: An integrative theoretical model of reading disability. *Journal of Learning Disabilities, 27,* 91–103.

Sternberg, R. (1985). *Beyond IQ: A triarchic theory of human intelligence*. New York: Cambridge University Press.

Tharp, R., and Gallimore, R. (1988). *Rousing minds to life: Teaching, learning, and schooling in social context*. Cambridge: Cambridge University Press.

Thorkildsen, T. (1989). Pluralism in children's moral reasoning about social justice. *Child Development, 60,* 965–972.

Thorne, B. (1993). Gender play: Girls and boys in school. New Brunswick, NJ: Rutgers University Press.

Vygotsky, L. (1978). *Mind in Society: The development of higher mental processes*. Cambridge, MA: Harvard University Press.

Walker, L., Hennig, K., and Krettenauer, T. (2000). Parent and peer contexts for children's moral reasoning development. *Child Development, 7,* 1033–1048.

Weiss, J., and Hagen, R. (1988). A key to literacy: Kindergarteners' awareness of the function of print. *The Reading Teacher, 41,* 574–578.

Wigfield, A., Ecles, J., Mac Iver, D., Reuman, D., and Midgeley (1991). Transitions during early adolescence: Changes in children's domain-specific self-perceptions and general self-esteem across the transition to junior high school. *Developmental Psychology, 27,* 552–565.

Wood, T., Cobb, P., and Yackel, E. (1992). Change in learning mathematics: Change in teaching mathematics. In H. Marshall (ed.), *Redefining student learning: Roots of educational change*. Norwood, NJ: Ablex.

Socioemotional Development and Motivation in the Classroom

CHAPTER PREVIEW

This chapter is intended to provide child study students with strategies to help them enter the social-emotional realm of the child in the classroom. It begins with a look at children's understanding of self and others, proceeds with a look at children's relationships with teachers and classmates, and concludes with a look at the larger picture of social support and motivational features of the classroom environment. The interviews and observations allow insights into children's adjustment and motivation to learn in school; suggestions for creating individual child profiles based on such insights are provided in Chapter 6.

SOCIAL COGNITION

Social cognition is defined as the understanding of self and others, including the understanding of feelings, thoughts, beliefs, and psychological dispositions. The child may be seen as a "budding personality theorist" (Selman, 1981) or "folk psychologist " (Olson & Burner, 1996). Children's social cognitions often explain and influence their motivated behavior and social interactions; thus, it is important for educators to become aware of ways to tap them. In this section, strategies are provided to reveal children's understandings of facial expressions and emotions, self-concepts, and others' dispositions.

CONTENTS

Understanding of Emotions

As children enter early and middle childhood, their expanded social experiences and cognitive capacities provide rich opportunities for developing social competencies. One of the important social competencies developed is the ability to identify and understand their own and others' emotional expressions and states (e.g., Harris, 1989; Saarni, Mumme, & Campos, 1998). This competency has been associated with greater peer acceptance (Cassidy et al., 1992). A significant source of information and communication is the facial expressions of others. For example, a child receives cues about how teachers and classmates feel about his or her behavior and performance from their expressions (e.g., Babad, Bernieri, & Rosenthal, 1991).

The following strategy (Strategy 5.1) may be used to study children's recognition of facial expressions of emotion and identification of emotions. It is adapted from methods used by researchers to examine the development of emotional understanding in early and middle childhood (e.g., Izard, 1972; Odom & Lemond, 1972). Before using this strategy, interviewers should review the guidelines presented in Chapter 2 for helping children feel comfortable and encourage them to attend to the task.

STRATEGY

5.1 | *Identifying Facial Expressions and Emotions*

Ages 4–11

Participants: Interview at least two children from each of the following age groups: (a) 4–5 years, (b) 6–8 years, (c) 9–11 years

Materials: Photographs of children and/or adults depicting eight different facial expressions of emotion. See Figure 5.1 for sample photographs.

Procedure:

Part 1: Place the eight photographs of children (or adults) depicting different emotions in front of the child. Ask the child to "show me the child (or adult) who is/has _____." Complete the statement by referring to each of the events described below (in random order). Record the number of times (0, 1, or 2) that the child accurately *recognized the expression* in the chart below.

Part 2: Show the eight photographs of children (or adults) depicting different emotional expressions again, point to one of the photographs and ask the child to "tell me how you think that this person feels." Record whether or not the child provided an accurate *expression label* on the record form; you may note whether the label given was approximate ("yucky" for disgust) or exact.

Part 3: Ask the child to "tell me how someone might feel who _____." Complete the stem by referring to each of the events below in random order. (Interviewers may adapt or add event descriptions.) Record the number of times (0, 1, or 2) the child responds with the appropriate *emotion label* in the chart.

Expression	*Event (adapted from Odom & Lemond, 1972)*
Fear	... being chased by a mean dog
	... running away from a strange man
Anger	... getting ready to hit somebody
	... seen somebody take a favorite toy (CD) away
Distress/Sad	... fallen down and skinned his/her knee
	... seeing a dog or cat get run over by a car
Shame	... gotten caught doing something bad
	... dumped school papers all over the floor in class
Disgust	... stepped in dog poop
	... found a smashed bug in his/her milk
Surprise	... seen rain on a sunny day
	... seen an air balloon land on the playground
Joy/Happy	... gotten a big bowl of ice cream
	... gotten a cute puppy for his/her birthday
Interest	... watching a rocket take off
	... watching a good TV program

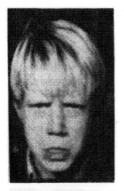 **ANGER**
 **DIGUST**
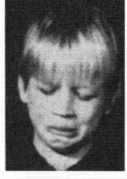 **DISTRESS**
 **FEAR**

 **INTEREST**
 **JOY**
 **SHAME**
 **SURPRISE**

Figure 5.1
Facial expressions.

Record Form 5.1: Identifying Facial Expressions and Emotions

	Happy	Sad	Fear	Anger	Disgust	Surprise	Interest	Shame
Total Child 1: Age _____								
Recognize Expression								
Label Expression								
Label Emotion								
Explain Cause								
Child 2: Age _____								
Recognize Expression								
Label Expression								
Label Emotion								
Explain Cause								
Child 3: Age _____								
Recognize Expression								
Label Expression								
Label Emotion								
Explain Cause								
Total Appropriate Responses:								

Adaptation: Drawing Facial Expressions

Prepare a page showing eight blank faces (circles) with different emotion labels. Ask children to complete each face by drawing what it would look like feeling _____ (happy, sad, afraid, angry, disgusted, surprised, interested, ashamed). (Read the emotion labels to young children.)

Additional Interview Questions: Causal Explanations

Children's abilities to provide reasonable causes for emotions experienced by self and others also may be studied by asking open-ended questions, such as "Tell me what would make you [your friend, teacher, etc.] feel happy [sad, disgusted, etc.]." Record the child's explanations (exact words, if possible) on a separate page and determine whether each explanation appears to match the emotion (see Chapter 2 for how to compare your judgments with another's and calculate agreement scores). Record the number of explanations judged appropriate in the chart above.

Interpreting Responses and Observations

Through examining the completed chart, you may have noted some general patterns in children's responses similar to those found in previous research. For example, researchers have found that young children can recognize and explain some basic emotions (happy, sad, anger, fear); children are better able to recognize than provide the label for expressions; and older children are better able to correctly identify and label emotional expressions than younger children (e.g., Harris, 1989; Izard, 1972).

You also may have noted that some children appear better able to correctly identify, label, and explain emotions than others, regardless of their age. Children's cognitive abilities and social experiences play a role in their understandings of emotions; thus, they continue to develop complex understandings of their own and others' emotional lives during middle childhood (e.g., Harter & Whitesell, 1989). Children from different settings also may demonstrate more or less sophisticated understandings of emotions. For example, some teachers may emphasize enhancing children's understandings of their own and others' emotions as a recognized curricular goal. It may be of interest to examine children's emotional awareness in such classrooms.

The content of children's explanations for their own and others' emotions may be analyzed for themes (see Chapter 2 for developing coding systems). For example, achievement or interpersonal themes may be seen in older children's explanations (Strayer, 1986). Such themes may indicate children's intensified concerns with achievement and peer relations in middle childhood (e.g., Erikson, 1950; Sullivan, 1953). These concerns also may be reflected in children's self-descriptions revealed in the next interview.

———✦✦✦———

SELF-CONCEPT

Self-concept refers to the beliefs, attitudes, knowledge, and impressions individuals have about themselves. Educators may be interested in studying children's self-concepts as a way to better understand their adjustment, learning, and performance in school, to better adapt instruction for them, or to become better acquainted with them as individuals. The following strategy is designed to reveal aspects of the child's self-concept. It incorporates questions and probes adapted from Damon and Hart's (1982, 1988) research on self-understanding in childhood and adolescence.

STRATEGY
••

5.2   *Self-Descriptions*

Ages 4–14

Participants: Interview at least two children from each of the following age groups: (a) 4–6 years, (b) 7–9 years, (c) 10–14 years.

Procedures: Start with the open-ended core questions listed below, and then follow with probes as needed to encourage children to expand upon their reasoning. Continue with suggested sample questions and your own follow-up questions until

Record Form 5.2: Self-Descriptions

	Child Age 4–6	Child Age 7–9	Child Age 10–14
Gender			
Age			
Group Membership			
Preferences/Interests			
Activities			
Physical Characteristics			
Personality			
Competencies			
Interpersonal Character			
Beliefs, Values			
Other			

children repeat themselves, say "I don't know" several times, or show signs of waning attention or frustration.

Core Questions: Tell me about yourself. What are you like?

What kind of person are you? What are you not like?

Sample Probes: What does that say about you? Why is that important? What differences does that (characteristic) make? What would be the difference if you were (were not) like that?

How would others (parents, friends) describe you? Do you agree with this description?

Adaptation: Paper-and-Pencil Method

Self-descriptions from children ages nine and above also can be elicited by using a simple paper-and-pencil method, such as the Twenty Statements Test (Bugental & Zelen, 1950) used in early studies of self-understanding (e.g., Montemayor & Eisen, 1977). To develop the form, write "Who am I?" 20 times and leave space for students to write a brief description after each question. Ask children to write 20 different responses if they can. This strategy can be used to collect responses from a group of children simultaneously.

Adaptation: Self-in-Context

To explore contextual influences on self-descriptions, the questions above can be adapted by simply asking children to describe themselves in their major social contexts, such as at school, at home, and with friends (Bronfenbrenner, 1979; Bronfenbrenner & Morris, 1998). For example, one may ask, "What are you like at school?" and follow with appropriate probes.

Coding and Recording Responses

First, organize the responses into meaningful categories and provide operational definitions when needed (see Chapter 2). For example, Montemayor and Eisen (1977) developed 30 categories to classify older elementary and high school students' responses to "Who am I?" questions. Sample categories are gender; age; student role; membership in social or ethnic group; judgments, tastes, likes; possessions, resources; physical self, body image; personality; sense of self-determination; sense of competence; sense of moral worth; interpersonal style; activities (artistic, physical, intellectual, other); ideological and belief references; and uncodable responses.

The next step is to assign each response to a category. A reliability check should be conducted by having a classmate or colleague assign a portion of the responses to appropriate categories and calculating agreement scores (see Chapter 2). Finally, develop a chart listing categories on one side and ages of children interviewed at the top, and complete it by recording the number of times children from a particular age group provide self-description related to the category (see sample response chart).

Interpreting Responses and Observations

Examine your completed chart for possible age-related differences in self-descriptions. You may note some developmental trends found in previous research. For example, studies have shown that young children focus on their physical characteristics, interests, and activities; older children (elementary age) add personality characteristics and competencies (e.g., friendly, good athlete) to such descriptions; and young adolescents include interpersonal characteristics, values, beliefs, and attitudes (e.g., Damon & Hart, 1982; Harter, 1998).

Examine the actual statements children used to describe themselves. You may note that some children described how they compared with others (e.g., "I am the best reader in the class). Researchers have found that children increasingly use social comparison information as they get older (e.g, Harter, 1998; Ruble, 1983). In addition, you may note that older children and adolescents described themselves differently across contexts, but expressed some discomfort with such differences (e.g., "I don't know why I'm so outgoing with friends, but shy in class"). Previous research has shown that older adolescents appear to be better able to integrate seemingly discrepant aspects of themselves than younger adolescents and children (e.g., Harter & Monsour, 1992).

Individual children's self-descriptions also may be summarized in separate reports, and used in conjunction with other interview responses and observations of behavior, to provide a glimpse into their self-concepts. Educators may use such "glimpses" into their students' self-concepts to provide ideas for adapting instructional activities to meet their needs and interests (e.g., Renninger, 1998).

———❖❖❖———

Perceptions of Competence

An important component of self-understanding is the evaluation of one's abilities. Developmental and educational psychologists are particularly concerned with children's perceptions of their competencies or abilities in school because such perceptions are related to their motives and efforts to learn and other achievement-related behaviors (e.g., Deci, & Ryan, 1985; Dweck & Leggett, 1988; Eccles, Wigfield, & Schiefele, 1998; Harter, 1983; Stipek & MacIver, 1989; Weiner, 1985). Studies of children's perceived competence often address two related questions: How do children define or conceptualize abilities or competencies? And How do they perceive their own abilities or competencies? The following strategy (Strategy 5.3) can be used to reveal children's conceptions and perceptions of competencies.

STRATEGY

Perceptions of Competence

Ages 5 to 10

Participants: Interview at least two children from each of the following age groups: (a) 5–6 years, (b) 7–8 years, (c) 9–10 years.

Materials: Create 5–point pictorial scales like the one depicted below by drawing one star with the label 1 beneath, two stars with the label 2, and so on.

*	**	***	****	*****
1	2	3	4	5

Procedure: Ask children (individually) to show you how "smart" and competent at tasks they think they are by pointing to or marking the appropriate number of stars. First explain the rating scale: "5 means that you are very smart (good at ____), 4 means that you are pretty smart (good at _____), 3 means that you are okay, 2 means that you are not very smart (good at __), and 1 means that you are not at all smart (good at _____)." Then ask children to choose the appropriate response to the following questions, and explain each choice in turn. Substitute words in parentheses for kindergartners if appropriate.

Questions:

How smart do you think you are?

How good at reading (letters) are you?

How good at math (numbers) are you?

How good at art are you? Sports (gym)? Other relevant subject areas?

Follow-up: How do you know? (How can you tell?) Why did you say that you were _____ ? Probe: Does it have something to do with the way you look? act? do things? think?

Adaptation: Expectations

You also may be interested in exploring children's expectations for the future. To do this, simply revise the questions as follows: How smart (good at ___) do you think you will be next year? You may want to help children focus on the future by engaging them in a brief discussion about the following year before you ask these questions. For example, you might ask them who their teachers and classmates might be, what activities they expect to participate in, and where their classrooms might be located.

Adaptation: Surveys for Older Children and Adolescents

The questions above can be included in a written survey for children ages 10 and above. Some of the questions may be modified to refer to grade-appropriate subject areas (e.g., substitute English for reading). Pictures (of stars) can be removed from the rating scales, and replaced with point descriptions in writing (i.e., not at all _____ , not _____ , okay _____, pretty _____ , very _____). Older children and adolescents can be asked to circle the number indicating their choice and explain each rating in writing; follow-up interviews with the child can be conducted to elaborate on explanations.

Coding Responses

The following categories may be used to describe children's understandings of competencies and abilities (e.g., Stipek, 1981; Yussen & Kane, 1985). You may want to create different categories and/or operational definitions to better represent your participants' responses (see Chapter 2).

Task Performance/Academic Skills (e.g., "I/he/she can...." "Gets A's (stars) on tests")

Work Habits/Effort (e.g., "s/he works hard," "finishes on time")

Knowledge (e.g., "knows ABCs," "multiplication tables")

Mental Processes (thinking, problem-solving, e.g., "figures out answers")

Social Behavior/Skills/Relationships (e.g., "gets along with others," "is nice")

Feedback from Others (e.g., "teacher (Mom) says so")

Tautological (repeats rating without offering further explanation, e.g., "just pretty smart")

Irrelevant (appears not to relate to question asked, e.g., "has a house," "likes worms")

Other (relevant, but does not fit the categories above, e.g., "good at football)

Interpreting Responses and Observations

If you noted that the youngest children in your sample responded that they were very smart and competent across subject areas or domains, your findings are consistent with previous research. Young children in kindergarten and first grade tend to be optimistic and have inflated perceptions of their own abilities; this optimism begins to gradually decline across the elementary and middle school years (e.g., Eccles, Wigfield, & Schiefele, 1998; Stipek & MacIver, 1989). You also may have noticed that younger children provided some irrelevant (from an adult perspective) or tautological responses and referred more frequently to work habits/effort and social behavior than older children (e.g., Nicholls, 1978; Stipek, 1998). Children of all ages interviewed are expected to be able to discriminate between their abilities in different domains (e.g., math, reading, sports) (e.g., Eccles, Wigfield, and Schiefele, 1998).

Classroom practices and other external factors influence children's perceived abilities, so it is also likely that you noted differences that were not related to age.

For example, even young children judge their abilities to be lower (or more realistic) in academic programs stressing evaluation (e.g., Stipek & Daniels, 1988; Stipek et al., 1995, 1998). Children with positive perceptions of competence are more likely to pursue, enjoy, persist, and perform better on challenging school tasks than those with low perceptions of competence (e.g., Dweck, 1999; Eccles, Wigfield, & Schiefele, 1998; Stipek, 1998); thus, it is critical for educators to attend to their students' perceived abilities. The final strategy presented in this chapter (Strategy 5.14) will guide observations of classroom practices that have implications for how children perceive their abilities.

Perceptions of Others' Dispositions

Children's views of the predictability of others' behavior (dispositions and reputations) have important implications for how they interact with others, including classmates and teachers (e.g., Dweck, 1999). The following strategy (Strategy 5.4) is intended to provide interviewers with insight into children's perspectives on others' behavior and dispositions and how these perspectives may differ from adults' views. Researchers often use prediction methods for examining children's understandings of others' personalities or dispositions (e.g., Gnepp & Chilumkurti, 1988; Heller & Berndt, 1981; Rholes, Newman, & Ruble, 1990); this strategy is adapted from one such study (Stipek & Daniels, 1990).

STRATEGY

Predicting Hypothetical Classmates' Behavior

Ages 5–14

Participants: Select at least two children from each of the following age groups: (a) 5–6 years, (b) 7–8 years, (c) 9–10 years, (d) 11–14 years.

Materials: Simple drawings of four hypothetical students. Objects, toys, or pictures representing two age-appropriate activities in each of the following domains: academic (e.g., book, puzzle), social (e.g., sharing, helping), physical (e.g., jumprope, drawing task). (Props are only needed for the youngest age groups.)

Procedure: Show drawings or provide brief physical descriptions of four hypothetical classmates (the same age as the child interviewed). Tell the child to pretend that one student is smart, one is not smart, one is nice, and one is not nice. Then ask the child to predict how well each of these students would probably perform or behave in various academic, social, and physical activities (see list of suggestions) by choosing the appropriate response depicted on four-point or pictorial scales like the following:

1	2	3	4
*	**	***	****
not well at all	just okay	well	very well

Record Form 5.4: Predicting Hypothetical Classmates' Behavior

	Smart	Not Smart	Nice	Not Nice
	Academic Social Physical	Academic Social Physical	Academic Social Physical	Academic Social Physical
Child Age 5–6				
Child Age 7–8				
Child Age 9–10				
Child Age 11–14				

Academic Activities: How well would _____ (each of the four students) do at reading a book? solving a puzzle? (Show or describe appropriate tasks.)

Social Activities: How well would _____ (each of the four students) do at sharing _____? Helping others _____? (Show or describe appropriate tasks.)

Physical Activities: How well would _____ (each of the four students) do at jumping over _____ ? Drawing _____ ? (Show or describe appropriate tasks.)

Recording and Interpreting Responses and Observations

Add the two prediction scores within each activity domain (academic, social, physical) for each hypothetical student, and use these combined prediction scores to complete the chart above. In examining the completed chart, you may have noted trends found in research on children's perceptions of others' dispositions or traits (e.g., Stipek & Daniels, 1990, Ruble & Dweck, 1995). The younger children in your sample may have predicted large performance or behavior differences between the "smart" and "not smart" student, and the "nice" and "not nice" student. In addition, younger children may have predicted similar differences across domains (e.g., the smart student received higher scores than the not smart student on all activities). In contrast, older children may have been more discriminating and predicted differences between students only in activities relevant to the disposition. For example, they might have predicted that the "smart" student would perform better than the "not smart" student in academic activities, but not necessarily in social and physical activities. Likewise, older children may have predicted that the "nice" student would demonstrate better social skills (e.g., sharing, helping) than the "not nice" student, but not better academic or physical skills.

Some developmental psychologists propose that children's judgments about others' dispositions (global or distinctive) may have important implications for their peer relationships and self-concepts (e.g., Erdley & Dweck, 1993; Rholes, Newman, & Ruble, 1990). Children who judge a classmate's behavior positively or negatively, for example, may form a general impression of the classmate and act in accordance with this impression (i.e., approach or avoid the classmate). This approach or avoidance behavior could, in turn, affect the classmate's self-concept and behavior in such a way to escalate a "good" or "bad" reputation. Teachers' responses to students can counter or feed into this process (e.g., White & Kistner, 1992; White & Jones, in press). In the next section, strategies for looking at teacher-student interactions and relationships are presented.

———✦✦✦———

STUDENT-TEACHER RELATIONSHIPS AND INTERACTIONS

Children's relationships with teachers in the elementary and middle grades influence their adjustment to school and their motives and attitudes toward learning (e.g., Birch & Ladd, 1997; Midgley, Feldlaufer, & Eccles, 1989; Pianta, 1999; Pianta & Steinberg, 1992; Skinner & Belmont, 1993). Thus, it is important for educators and others working with children to attempt to see "the teacher" through the eyes of the child. Strategy 5.5 is recommended to reveal children's perceptions of teachers and their desirable qualities in general. Strategy 5.6 includes several questions suggested for eliciting children's views of their own relationships with teachers (e.g., Pianta, 1999). Note that some young children may have difficulty responding to some of these interview questions in words. Therefore, do not be surprised if a five- or six-year-old child replies "I don't know." Other ways to tap young children's perceptions of teachers are suggested (see "Adaptations for Young Children" in Strategy 5.6).

STRATEGY

What Is a Good Teacher?

Ages 5–14

Participants: Interview at least two children from each of the following age groups: (a) 5–7 years, (b) 8–10 years, (c) 11–14 years.

Procedure: Begin with general open-ended questions and follow with probing questions like those suggested below. Inform the child that you are interested in his/her ideas about *any* teacher, not just his/her own teacher.

Interview Questions: What is a good teacher? What is he or she like? What if she or he were not like this? What is a not very good teacher like? Probes: What does he or she do? Act like? Say? Feel like? Think like?

Possible Categories for Responses: You may want to assign children's responses to the following categories and/or develop some of your own.

Caring/Warm/Friendly

Responsive (provides academic assistance/feedback when requested)

Interesting (provides stimulating lessons, activities, etc.)

Fair (distributes rewards, attention, etc. in a fair manner)

Individualizes Instruction (provides appropriate challenge, choices, flexible)

Record Form 5.5: Qualities of a Good Teacher

	Caring		Responsive		Interesting		Ind Inst.		Fair		Personal		Manager		Other	
	+	-	+	-	+	-	+	-	+	-	+	-	+	-	+	-
Child 1																
Child 2																
Child 3																

Personal (knows students as individuals with different backgrounds and interests)

Manages Classroom (provides clear instructions and appropriate structures for maintaining discipline and accomplishing tasks)

Other

Coding and Recording Responses

Children's responses to questions about teacher qualities in general may be assigned to the suggested categories and/or other categories you deem appropriate for describing your data (see Chapter 2). To examine similarities and differences in children's views of teachers, you may want to develop and complete a chart like the one in Record Form 5.5. Note the number of times that each child referred to a particular quality, indicating whether the quality is a positive (+) or a negative (-) characteristic or behavior.

Interpreting Responses and Observations

Because this technique relies heavily on children's abilities to express themselves in words, you may have noted that older children described more teacher qualities than did younger children. Other than this, you may not have observed any age-related differences in children's responses. Research conducted with elementary students (e.g., Daniels, Kalkman, & McCombs, 2001; Weinstein, 1983) and middle grade students (e.g., Wentzel, 1997) has shown similarities in children's descriptions of desirable teacher characteristics across grade levels.

It is important to acknowledge that children can and do reflect upon teacher behavior and qualities, and to discover what qualities matter to them. Children's perceptions of teachers affect their attitudes toward school and perceptions of themselves as learners (e.g., Perry & Weinstein, 1998).

The next strategy is designed to elicit children's perceptions of their own relationship with their teacher. Because this interview contains some sensitive questions, it is especially important to discuss ethical considerations with your instructor before proceeding (also see ethics section in Chapter 2). Do not conduct this interview if teachers or parents feel uncomfortable having others ask their children such personal questions. An alternative strategy is to adapt the questions to focus on relationships between teachers and students in general.

STRATEGY

5.6   *Quality of Relationship with Teacher*

Ages 5–14

Participants: Interview at least two children from each of the following age groups: (a) 5–7 years, (b) 8–10 years, (c) 11–14 years.

Procedure: Inform the child that you are interested in finding out what he or she feels about his or her teacher. Assure him or her that you are studying what children of different ages think about teachers, and that you will not tell anyone what he or she says. If the child has several teachers, ask the child to think about the teacher he or she spends the most time with (e.g., the homeroom teacher).

Sample Questions (first four questions are adapted from Pianta, 1999):

1. What are some things this teacher does that makes you feel good? Like school? What are some other things that your teacher does to make you feel good in the classroom? How often does this happen?

2. If you are feeling upset about something, can your teacher help you feel better? How? Can you tell me about a time that this happened?

3. Does this teacher pay much attention to you? What do you do to get him or her to pay attention to you?

4. Does this teacher help you with schoolwork when you need it? How does she or he help you and the other students in the class?

5. How much do think this teacher cares about you? Children can indicate response on a four-point scale:

*	**	***	****
not much	a little	pretty much	a lot

How do you know? (How can you tell?)

6. How important is it to you that your teacher cares about you?

*	**	***	****
not important	a little	pretty important	very important

Why is it _____ important to you?

Adaptation for Young Children

To assist young children and children with limited verbal skills who may have difficulty responding to open-ended questions, you may want to adapt some questions and develop simple response options. For example, one could ask: "How good does your teacher make you feel most of the time?" and ask children to respond by pointing to the appropriate drawing of a face:

big frown	small frown	small smile	big smile
"not good at all"	"just okay"	"pretty good"	"very good"

Interpreting Responses and Observations

The purpose of this interview was not to examine similarities and differences between children's responses, but to look carefully at individual children's "models" or "portraits" of their relationships with their own teachers. You may have formed an impression of a child's perceptions of teacher support that may help explain his or her attitudes toward school learning (e.g., Birch & Ladd, 1997; Midgley, Feldlaufer, & Eccles, 1989; Pianta, 1999; Pianta & Steinberg, 1992; Skinner & Belmont, 1993). You may want to reflect on this impression in connection with an observation of the child's interactions with the teacher (Strategy 5.7).

The following strategy utilizes event-sampling to focus on particular children's interactions with teachers (see introduction to event samples in Chapter 2). Before conducting observations, expand on the descriptions of the behaviors below (in collaboration with classmates or colleagues) and develop a record sheet with five event samples for each child observed (see sample below).

——‡‡‡——

STRATEGY

Observations of Teacher-Student Interactions

Ages 4–14

Participants: Select one or two children from a class in each of the following grades: (a) PreK–2, (b) 3–5, (c) 6–8.

Procedure: Observe children during times that they are likely to have many opportunities to interact with teachers. Record the behavior of the target child whenever she or he initiates an interaction with the teacher or receives an initiative (bid) from the teacher. You may use the following categories to characterize initiations, responses, and the affective tone of the response. Your observations may be simiply recorded on a form like the one shown. Continue observing until you have collected data on five interaction events per child (this may require another visit).

Bids for Attention (Initiator: Teacher or Child)

Touch:	Touches shoulder, clothing
Name:	Calls name
Talks:	Makes statement (e.g., I did my homework)
Position:	Places object or self near a person (too near to be ignored)
Requests:	Asks for help or assistance or attention
Demands:	Demands attention loudly and assertively
Disrupts:	Behaves in manner to disrupt ongoing activity
Other:	For example, raises hand

Responses to Bid

Immediate:	Responds within a few seconds
Delay:	Responds later (estimate time)
Ignores:	Does not respond

Record Form 5.7: Observations of Teacher-Student Interaction

Target Child _____

Event #1: Setting_____ Date _____ Time _____

   Initiator: Teacher _____ Child _____

   Bid: Touch ____ Name _____ Talk _____ Position _____

   Request _____ Demand _____ Disrupt _____ Other _____

Brief Description:

Response: Immediate _____ Delay _____ Time: ____ Ignore _____

   Affect: Positive _____ Neutral _____ Negative _____

Brief Description:

Affective Tone of Response

Positive: Response characterized by warmth and respect (e.g., smiles)

Neutral: Response appears neither positive nor negative

Negative: Response characterized by negative tone (e.g., anger, frustration, aloofness) or disrespect

Interpreting Observations

Observers may use event sampling to note patterns in student-teacher interactions. In this case, you may have noted a tendency for some children or teachers to initiate most of the interactions. You also may have noted some consistency in the emotional quality of reactions. Of course, one would have more confidence in such observations if they were conducted across time and settings (e.g., not just on Monday morning when the students are tired and the teacher is grumpy) and showed high interobserver agreement (see Chapter 2). Such observations may provide ideas for improving teacher-child relationships. For example, educators may discover that they attend more to certain children who initiate and respond favorably to their own initiatives, and decide to use this information to direct their interactions to noninitiators. This decision may be particularly important for helping withdrawn or neglected children (see your child development text and next section).

———

PEER RELATIONSHIPS, PLAY, AND SCHOOL ADJUSTMENT

Relationships with peers and friends play a critical role in children's adjustment to school (e.g., Asher & Coie, 1990; Berndt & Keefe, 1992; Eccles, Wigfield, and Schiefele, 1998; Ladd,

1996). Children who are accepted by peers are more likely to succeed academically as well as demonstrate positive attitudes toward learning and school (e.g., Damon, 1984; Ladd, 1996; Savin-Williams & Berndt, 1990). In this section, strategies for looking at peer relations and friendships from the child's perspective will be presented, followed by strategies for examining opportunities for social interaction and development of social skills in the classroom and other school settings (e.g., playground, lunchroom, afterschool programs).

Views of Friendship and Peer Relationships

The following strategy incorporates common questions asked by researchers to reveal children's conceptions of friendship. Suggestions for classifying the children's responses are given, along with brief category descriptions. Before assigning responses, expand on the operational definitions of each category through examining children's friendship descriptions obtained by previous researchers (refer to your child development text) and by discussing them with your own classmates or colleagues. You also may add categories that better represent your participants' responses. (See Chapter 2 for additional hints on developing and defining coding categories.)

STRATEGY

5.8   *What Is a Friend?*

Ages 5–14

Participants: Interview at least two children from each of the following age groups: (a) 5–7 years, (b) 8–10 years, (c) 11–14 years.

Procedure: Tell the child that you are interested in hearing about his/her ideas about friends.

Sample Interview Questions

1. What is a friend? Or: Tell me about a friend of yours and why he or she is your friend. Probes: What is important about that? If a person was not like this, would he or she still be a friend?
2. Why is it nice to have friends? Probes: How does it feel to have a friend? Not have a friend? Is it important to have lots of friends? Or just one? Why?
3. How can you tell that someone is a best friend? Probe: How is this different from just a friend?

Sample Categories

Playmate (someone to engage in activities with)

Companion (someone to be with, like, enjoy)

Prosocial (someone to be nice to, do things for, help, not fight with)

Intimacy (someone to share secrets with or discuss problems with, self-disclose)

Record Form 5.8: Children's Views of Friends

	Playmate	Companion	Reciprocal	Prosocial	Intimacy	Loyal	Support	Other
Child Age ____								
Child Age ____								
Child Age ____								

Loyal/Trustworthy (someone to "stick up" for you, "not talk behind your back")

Reciprocal (someone who considers you a friend)

Supports Self (someone who makes you feel good about yourself)

Other

Recording and Interpreting Observations

Complete the chart for Strategy 5.8 by recording whether the child described a characteristic or behavior that fits each category. If the children you interviewed responded similarly to participants in previous studies on conceptions of friendship, then you may have noted that the youngest child provided more descriptions in the first four categories (playmate, companion, prosocial, reciprocal) and the older children (above age 8) provided descriptions that fit the latter categories (intimacy, loyal, support) (e.g., Berndt, 1983; Rubin & Coplan, 1992).

The next strategy (Strategy 5.9) is an adaptation of a sociometric technique designed to gather information about the quality of children's relationships with peers. Children are often excellent at indicating who in their peer group has positive and negative relationships (i.e., who is popular, rejected, neglected) (Asher & Dodge, 1998; Rubin & Coplan, 1992).

———✦✦✦———

STRATEGY

Quality of Peer Relationships

Ages 5–14

Participants: Five to ten children from one class.

Procedure: Ask children, individually, to nominate classmates either by telling you in words or in writing. Assure children that you will not reveal their answers to anyone.

Questions

1. Name three students in your class that you like to play/do things with most of the time. Probe: Why do you play/do things with them? What do you do?
2. Name three students in your class that you don't play/do things with much at all. Probe: Why don't you play/do things with them?

Follow-up: Before children return to class, engage them in a brief discussion about the importance of not talking with classmates about their choices ("because it might hurt someone's feelings") and, perhaps, conduct a brief unrelated activity (e.g., card game) to distract them from the topic.

Adaptation: The Teacher's View

Teachers also can share their insights about children's relationships with peers. To reveal teachers' perspectives, ask them to (a) report (in words or writing) names of a few children in their class considered popular, unpopular (rejected), and neglected; and (b) describe social qualities of children in each group.

Recording and Interpreting Responses and Observations

Select classmates who were nominated more than once in the preferred and non-preferred groups and examine children's explanations for nominating these class-mates. Summarize the perceived social qualities of preferred and nonpreferred classmates. You may find that the preferred (potentially popular) classmates are depicted as fun, friendly, helpful, and the like; in contrast, nonpreferred (potentially rejected) classmates may be characterized as aggressive and disruptive. These summaries can be compared with detailed descriptions and discussions of children's social groups and behavior in your child development text. You also may want to compare children's descriptions of preferred classmates to their descriptions of friends gathered from conducting Strategy 5.8. Peers and friends play different but equally important roles and functions in children's social adjustment and socioemotional development (e.g., Buhrmester & Furman, 1986; Rubin, Bukowski, & Parker, 1998; Sullivan, 1953).

Finally, you may want to compare and contrast children's and teachers' nominations and descriptions. Previous research shows that teachers and their students often agree about the relative sociability and aggressiveness of classmates (i.e., preferred and rejected children nominated), but often disagree about who demonstrates withdrawn behavior until the later elementary grades (e.g., Rubin, Bukowski, and Parker, 1998; Rubin & Copland, 1992).

Although you cannot identify a child's social group without gathering more evidence, you may have gleaned, from nominations and descriptions, a general impression of some children who may be popular and others who may be rejected. Such information may be helpful for a teacher to ensure that all children in a class feel included and receive needed assistance with developing social skills and friendships. Feeling accepted by peers as well as by teachers is critical for healthy school adjustment and subsequent learning (e.g., Ladd, 1996; McCombs & Whisler, 1997; Wentzel & Asher, 1995).

Social Behavior

The purpose of the following observation strategy is to examine children's engagement in different kinds of play and social interactions. This time-sampling strategy incorporates characterizations of social activity used in previous research on children's play (e.g., Parten, 1932; Rubin & Coplan, 1992). We suggest conducting these observations in different school settings: in the classroom (during "free-choice" activities), on the playground, in the lunchroom, and, if possible, during after-school activities. Refer to Chapter 2 for more information on the use of time-sampling strategies.

Observers must clearly define the social behavior categories and recognize characteristic behaviors before utilizing this time-sampling technique. We recommend the following preparatory steps: (a) write operational definitions (refer to descriptions of social behavior in child development texts); (b) conduct preliminary observations of behavior to check the appropriateness of the category descriptions (e.g., observe elementary students during a half-hour of free-play); and (c) revise category descriptions. It may be worthwhile for several student observers to compare notes during this preparation phase.

STRATEGY

5.10   *Observations of Social Interactions and Play*

Ages 4–10

Participants: Select five children from a primary class (grades K-2) and five children from an upper elementary class (grades 3–5).

Materials: Bring stopwatch, clipboard, category descriptions, and four code sheets.

Procedure:

Primary Class: Observe a selected child for one minute, and assign his or her behavior to one of the categories on a code sheet like the one shown below by making a check mark in the appropriate space. Follow the same procedure with the other four children selected. Repeat the procedure until you have observed each of the selected children for five minutes in two different settings (10 minutes total per child).

Elementary Class. Observe five children in two settings using the same procedure as described above.

Adaptation: Focus on Individuals

The categories below also can be used to observe one child at a time for consecutive time intervals (ranging from seconds to minutes) across settings for the purpose of identifying or documenting particularly sociable, aggressive, or withdrawn behavior (e.g., Rubin & Coplan, 1992). You may want to select preferred and nonpreferred classmates identified in Strategy 5.9 to support or disconfirm children's and/or teachers' impressions.

Adaptation: Opportunities for Social Interaction

This observation strategy also can be adapted for the purpose of examining opportunities for social interaction in a class. To accomplish this, you could make a list of all of the chil-

Record Form 5.10: Social Behavior in Different Settings

Grade Level: _____   Setting: Classroom   Playground   Lunchroom   Other _____

Time: _____

	Child 1	Child 2	Child 3	Child 4	Child 5
Gender:	M F	M F	M F	M F	M F

Social Behavior Categories:

Unoccupied

Onlooker

Conversation
(specify: adult or child)

Play (specify: Solitary,
Parallel, or Group)

   Sensorimotor

   Exploratory

   Constructive

   Dramatic

   Games-with-Rules

   Rough and Tumble

Aggression

Prosocial (helping,
sharing–nonacademic)

Tutor (assist with
academic work)

Other (describe)

dren in one class across the top of the code sheet, observe each child for 10 seconds, and record the various types of social activities children engage in periodically throughout the school day (e.g., every hour). You may want to observe children from another class using the same procedure and compare types of social engagement across classes.

Recording and Interpreting Observations

One purpose for this observation is to enhance awareness of the kinds of social behavior children of different ages and characteristics display. For example, by examining the number of check marks across code sheets, you may have noticed that the older children engaged in more gamelike activities and conversations and less dramatic and rough-and-tumble play with peers than younger children (e.g., Rubin, Bukowski, and Parker, 1998). In addition, you may have noticed that boys engaged in more aggressive activities than girls (e.g., Coie & Dodge, 1998).

If you decided to adapt the strategy to focus on individual children, you may have noticed unoccupied, onlooker, and parallel play behaviors indicative of a withdrawn child, aggressive behaviors indicative of a rejected child, and prosocial and other active play behaviors indicative of a popular child (e.g., Rubin & Coplan, 1992). If observers, teachers, and peers consistently identify the same children as having difficulties with peer relations over time, it would be important for trained school personnel to help these children develop social skills, especially those rejected (refer to your child development text for information about problems related to peer rejection).

Finally, you may have noticed differences in the types of social behaviors that children displayed in different contexts and/or classrooms. School and classroom policies vary in the extent that opportunities for social interactions are valued and made available. Children may be better able to develop social competencies and relationships when safe and ample opportunities for social interaction are provided.

———❖❖❖———

Social Support and School Adjustment

School adjustment is defined as "the degree to which children become interested, engaged, comfortable, and successful in the school environment" (Ladd, 1996, p. 371). Children's adjustment to school is partly dependent on the extent to which they receive support from teachers, parents, and classmates. Some developmental psychologists propose that children's relationships with classmates may be among the most important sources of support (e.g., Goodenow, 1993; Ladd, 1990). In the previous section, strategies for revealing children's perceptions of teacher support were introduced. The strategy described below (Strategy 5.11) is intended to provide a glimpse into how children perceive the nature of their classmates' support. As with the teacher-support interview, this strategy contains some sensitive questions, thus it is important to discuss ethical considerations with your instructor before proceeding (also see ethics section in Chapter 2). An alternative strategy is to adapt the questions to focus on relationships between students in the class in general.

STRATEGY

Perceptions of Social Support

Ages 6–14

Participants: Select at least one child from each of the following age groups: (a) 6–7 years, (b) 8–10 years, (c) 11–14 years.

Materials: Create scales: pictorial (tower) rating scale for children under 10, scale points in writing for older children. (See sample in Figure 5.2.)

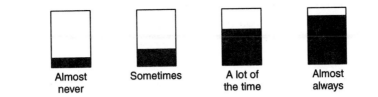

Figure 5.2
Sample Pictorial Rating Scale

Almost never   Sometimes   A lot of the time   Almost always

Procedure: Interview children individually. Explain that you will ask some questions about their feelings about the kids in their class (homeroom), and that you will not share their responses. Explain the rating scale to younger children by using an example like the following: Let's say I asked you if you liked to eat ice cream. Point to the tallest tower if your answer is "almost always," the next tower if your answer is "a lot of the time," the next tower if your answer is "sometimes," and the shortest tower if your answer is "almost never." Ask children to explain a few of their responses and tell you how they feel about how kids treat them.

Interview Questions

(appropriate wording for older children is included in parentheses):

1. Do kids in your class pay attention to you? Listen to you? (Notice your efforts?)
2. Do kids in your class act nice to you? Do nice things for you?
3. Do kids in your class spend time doing things with you? Play with you at recess? (Eat lunch with you?)
4. Do kids in your class help you with your schoolwork? Explain how to do things?
5. Do kids in your class say nice things to you? About your work? About how you look or act?
6. Do kids in your class choose you to be in their group or team?
7. What else can you tell me about how you feel about the kids in your class and how they treat you? Is the way these kids treat you important? Why?

Adaptation for Young Children

The first three interview questions above can be modified for four- and five-year-old children: Add the phrase "most of the time" to the question, and ask them to respond with either "yes" or "no." Some young children may be able to explain their response or provide an example.

Interpreting Responses and Observations

Children's responses should leave you with an impression or portrait of how they feel about their classmates' support. You are not expected to note systematic age differences in children's feelings about the importance of peer support in the classroom; research shows that such support is precious throughout the elementary and middle grades (e.g., Goodenow, 1993; Ladd, 1990). However, you may have noted conspicuous individual differences in children's perceptions of support (e.g., Asher & Coie, 1990). You may want to write these impressions in a brief paper, making references to the child's exact words whenever possible. Your impressions may be supported by observations and reports by peers and teachers previously obtained (using Strategy 5.9).

———✠✠✠———

CLASSROOM ENVIRONMENTS AND STUDENT MOTIVATION

Views of Schoolwork and Student Motivation

Educational psychologists study children's adjustment to school by examining their attitudes toward school learning and activities, as well as their perceptions of support, acceptance, and competence (e.g., Ladd, 1996; McCombs & Whisler, 1997; Perry & Weinstein, 1998). Children who are well-adjusted are more likely to learn and benefit from their school experiences (e.g., Ladd, 1996). The next interview strategy (Strategy 5.12) is designed to help educators look at children's views of schoolwork and their motives to learn. The youngest children may have difficulty answering some of these open-ended questions (particularly questions 5 and 6); suggestions for adapting the questions for use with less verbal children are provided below.

STRATEGY

Views of Schoolwork

Ages 6–14

Participants: Interview at least one child from each of the following grade levels: (a) 1–2, (b) 3–5, (c) 6–8.

Procedure: To initiate the interview, ask the child to tell you a few things about the *kinds* of schoolwork they do. Then proceed with asking general questions about how he feels about his schoolwork, using probing questions when needed to encourage elaboration (sample questions are given below). You can choose to focus on child's views of a particular subject area or of schoolwork in general (referring to a variety of subjects).

Sample Interview Questions:

1. What do you like about your schoolwork (math work, reading work, science)? Why? What do you not like? Why?

2. Why do you want to do well on your schoolwork? Probes: To learn? To please yourself? Your teacher? Your parents? Your friends? To get good grades? To do better than the other students? To not be embarrassed? To earn some reward (award, prize, privilege)? To get a job someday?

3. What schoolwork do you think is easy? Hard? Just right (in between-not too easy and not too hard)? Do you like the easy, hard, or just right work? Why?

4. What schoolwork do you think is interesting? Boring? Why?

   Probes: Does it make you think hard? work hard? or not so hard?

5. What schoolwork do you think is most important (matters most) for you to learn? Least important (doesn't matter) to learn? Why?

6. How can you *tell* if you have done your schoolwork well? or not so well? Probes: Do you figure it out yourself? How? Do you look at your grades? The teacher's marks on your papers? At how other students have done?

7. What else do you want to tell me about the work you do *or would like to do* in school?

Adaptation: Younger Children

Some elementary-age children may have difficulty reflecting on and/or communicating about their motives for learning in school. To capture young children's interests in their schoolwork, you may want to create a pictorial scale with stars and explain that five stars means "very interesting" ("like very much") and one star means "not at all interesting" ("do not like at all") (see Strategy 5.3 for details). You may devise simple questions such as, "How interesting is your schoolwork? Spelling? Math work?" or "How much do you like doing your schoolwork?" and ask children to point to the appropriate set of stars to show what they think. Some children may be able to explain their choices.

Interpreting Responses and Observations

You may have noted that young children, in general, expressed greater interest or intrinsic motivation in learning about academic school subjects than older children, especially in math and science (e.g., Eccles, Wigfield, and Schiefele, 1998). Older children and young adolescents may have made more references to performing well to "look good" rather than for the value and enjoyment of learning (e.g., Dweck, 1999; Stipek, 1998). (See your child development text for a discussion of performance/ego versus mastery/learning orientation.) On the other hand, you may have interviewed children whose interests in schoolwork appear to be closely tied to particular classroom activities and climate (teacher and classmate support). For example, we would expect children to enjoy schoolwork who feel they can do well, and have opportunities to engage in varied, novel, and somewhat challenging activities in a relatively noncritical, noncompetitive environment (see this chapter's *Resources*). The next two strategies provide ways to observe children's engagement in classroom activities, the teacher's structure of those activities, and the classroom climate in general.

Strategy 5.13, a time-sampling strategy, is designed to manifest the extent to which students are engaged in various academic learning tasks (adapted from Irwin & Bushnell, 1980). Before conducting this observation, it may be helpful to review the section on time-sampling in Chapter 2, as well as motivation theorists' descriptions of engaged or task-focused activity in your child development text. Csikszentmihalyi (1990), describes intense engagement in an activity or attention to a task as "flow." Individuals report that their best and most creative work is done in a flow state. Other researchers conceptualize engagement as the attention, interest, and effort expended to learn (e.g., Marks, 2000). In any case, engagement involves directed thought and emotions. As would be expected, students who are engaged in authentic school tasks demonstrate higher learning and achievement (e.g., Finn, 1989; Finn & Rock, 1997). You may want to revise or create your own categories and definitions of engagement before conducting this observation.

———※———

STRATEGY

 5.13 *Observation of Student Engagement*

Ages 4–14

Participants: Randomly select five children from a pre-K or primary classroom and five children from an upper elementary class (grades 3–5).

Materials: Bring several copies of code sheet and stopwatch.

Procedure: Observe each child for 10 minutes during instructional activities in at least two academic subject areas (e.g., reading, math). Record the number of minutes that the child engages in each of the following behaviors on a code sheet like the one in Record Form 5.13.

On-task: Attention to teacher, students, or materials related to an assigned or appropriate task

Off-task: Inattention to assigned or appropriate task

Engaged: Demonstrating thoughtful, focused attention or participation

Disruptive: Demonstrating inappropriate behavior

Adaptation: Focus on Individual Students

This strategy may be adapted to examine a particular student's engagement with tasks across time and settings. For example, if you were interested in trying to explain a child's motivation and/or performance in various academic subjects, you could observe the child's attention to these tasks periodically throughout the school day by revising the record chart (list different subject areas instead of different children). You might augment these observations by interviewing the child about his or her pursuit of academic interests in and outside the school setting (see Strategy 5.12).

Adaptation: Focus on Activities

This strategy also may be adapted to investigate effectiveness (or engagement level) of particular classroom activities for all students in a class. To observe all students, simply write all names along the side of the record chart, observe each for one minute, and check the best description of his or her task involvement during that minute. Complete the chart by finding the total number of children demonstrating various engagement levels.

Interpreting Responses and Observations

One would expect to note individual differences in engagement levels. Some children may carefully attend to most assigned tasks and others may be more discriminating and attend only to tasks they find interesting, relevant, and appropriately challenging (e.g., Ryan & Stiller, 1991; Stipek, 1998). Students in general are expected to demonstrate engagement when they are working on authentic, challenging tasks and feel a strong sense of social support (e.g., Marks, 2000). (See Strategies 5.6, 5.11). Thus, it is likely that you observed some classroom tasks that appear to engage more students than other tasks. It may be worthwhile to scrutinize these tasks in terms of their "match" or "mismatch" to the interests and abilities of the students (Strategies 5.3, 5.12) (see dis-

Record Form 5.13: Observation of Student Engagement

Time and Setting: _____

Activity/Task Description: _____

	On-Task & Engaged	On-Task, *Not* Engaged	Off-Task, *Not* Disruptive	Off-Task & Disruptive	Other: Describe
Child 1					
Child 2					
Child 3					
Child 4					
Child 5					
Total minutes					

cussion of motivation research in your child development text). Strategy 5.14 will help observers focus on the features of the classroom environment that influence student motivation to learn in school.

Classroom Environment

Educational psychologists have developed a variety of approaches to examine the classroom environment in the early, elementary, and middle grade levels (see *Resources* at the end of this chapter). The following observation strategy incorporates several major features of the environment related to the quality of student motivation and learning. Sample classroom description items are listed. Before initiating Strategy 5.14, observers are expected to clarify, revise, and prepare additional classroom description items in collaboration with classmates, colleagues, and instructors; this task may require preliminary classroom observations. Select one classroom from which you have interviewed and observed some of the children.

STRATEGY

Classroom Environment Survey

Grades PreK–8

Procedure: Observers must spend at least two hours observing activities in a classroom before completing their survey. Observations should be conducted during the time period that the teacher says most of the children are in the classroom partici-

Record Form 5.14: Classroom Environment Survey

Child Choice/Initiative

Children choose tasks from a variety of options, challenge levels.

Children choose who they want to work with.

Children choose how and where to conduct various tasks.

Children can work at their own pace.

Children can determine when they have completed a task or assignment.

Participation

Teacher encourages children to ask questions rather than listen passively.

Most children participate in class discussions.

Most children participate actively in class activities (i.e., appear engaged in tasks).

Affiliation/Cooperation

Children help each other, share materials.

Children appear to know their classmates well.

Children appear to enjoy working together.

Peer assistance (help) with tasks is encouraged.

Competition Emphasis

Children compete for teacher recognition.

Children compete for grades, rewards, or positive evaluation signs (e.g., stars on papers).

Children compete for peer recognition.

Inquiry Focus

Children find out answers to questions through own investigations.

Teacher emphasizes thinking skills and processes of inquiry.

Teacher provides clues, hints, examples to encourage problem-solving.

Teacher encourages creative or novel ideas.

Performance/Evaluation Emphasis

Individual student performance is salient (e.g., grades, "correct" and "incorrect" answers are publicized).

Teacher emphasizes comparison of student performance and behavior.

Praise and other rewards are given mainly to high achievers.

Classroom Management

There appears to be a clear set of rules for students to follow.

Teacher deals consistently with students who break rules.

Children appear to understand what they are expected to do.

Most children demonstrate positive behavior.

(continued on following page)

(continued from previous page)

Teacher Support

The teacher takes a personal interest in the students.

The teacher listens to and respects each child's point of view.

Teacher appears to have high expectations for all students to perform and behave.

Teacher attends appropriately to all students, not just a few.

Teacher appears to accept and be responsive to individual differences in students.

Classroom Materials/Displays

A variety of materials are available for children's use.

Displays show a variety of children's work .

Teacher Structure of Academic Tasks

There is evidence of modifications of academic tasks for individual or small groups of students.

Teacher presents instructional activities materials in a variety of forms (e.g., demonstration, discussion, brief lecture).

Teacher adjusts challenge level of tasks for individual students.

General Classroom Atmosphere

Children appear comfortable, relaxed (few appear tense or nervous).

Classroom atmosphere is *not* characterized by silence, tentative responding by children.

Classroom atmosphere is characterized by cheerful voices of children.

---

pating in the general education curriculum. Respond to each of the survey items by indicating how often the practice occurs on a scale like the following:

0	1	2	3	4	5
not observed	almost never	seldom	sometimes	often	very often

Interpreting Observations

Determine an average rating score for each feature of the environment (i.e., child choice, participation, affiliation). It is important to interpret these "scores" cautiously since your observations were conducted during a brief time period and may not be reliable (see Chapter 2). However, you may have formed an impression of some features of the classroom learning environment and atmosphere. You also may have noticed how some features of the environment appear to influence student attitudes, motives, and behavior. For example, one would expect to see many students engaged and demonstrate positive attitudes and behavior in a classroom characterized by opportunities for choice, active problem-solving, and participation with others within a well-managed, supportive atmosphere (e.g., Eccles, Wigfield, and Schiefele, 1998). In contrast, one would expect at least a few students to demonstrate negative attitudes and behavior in a classroom characterized by performance pressure, rigid tasks, and differential support of individuals. Of course, it is likely that you observed a classroom that is not clearly characterized as one or the other; in these cases, it is most important to consider the classroom from the perspective of the child.

—✛✛✛—

CHAPTER SUMMARY

Educators are expected to gain insights into how children understand, perceive, and feel about their roles in the classroom through the use of interview and observation strategies, such as those outlined in this chapter. Furthermore, it is expected that educators note how children's views may influence as well as be influenced by features of the classroom environment. Educators who become aware of children's views of themselves as learners, their relationships with classmates and teachers, and the learning environment itself are better prepared to meet children's social-emotional needs and, hence, foster their motivation to learn and achieve in school.

REFLECTION QUESTIONS

1. How might children's abilities to recognize others' emotions influence their self-perceptions and social competencies? How do teachers' facial expressions communicate information to students about their competencies and behavior? (Strategy 5.1)

2. How can changes in children's self-understanding impact their motivation to learn and achieve in school? How can educators use knowledge about individual students' self-concepts to tailor their instruction? (Strategies 5.2, 5.3)

3. How could children's expectations of and behavior toward others differ based on their understanding of differentiated vs. global dispositions? (Strategy 5.4)

4. How can children's expectations and preferences regarding teacher behavior affect their attitudes toward learning and school adjustment? (Strategies 5.5, 5.6)

5. How could educators use Strategy 5.7 routinely to monitor student-teacher interactions and foster positive relationships?

6. How are children's views of friendship and the quality of their relationships associated? How do these associations differ across age? How do children's friendships and relationships affect their academic learning and performance in school? (Strategies 5.8, 5.9)

7. How can educators use Strategy 5.10 or 5.11 to identify children's social competencies and supports as well as potential interventions needed? What changes in the school environment (e.g., schedule, activities) can be made to facilitate positive interactions among students?

8. How might educators use Strategy 5.12, 5.13, or 5.14 to improve classroom practices and foster student learning and adjustment?

RESOURCES

Dweck, C. (1999). *Self-theories: Their role in motivation, personality, and development.* Philadelphia, PA: Psychology Press.

Juvonen, J., & Wentzel, K. (1996). *Social motivation: Understanding children's school adjustment.* New York: Cambridge University Press.

McCombs, B., & Whisler, J. (1997). *The learner-centered classroom and school: Strategies for increasing student motivation and achievement.* San Francisco: Jossey-Bass.

Nicholls, J., and Hazzard, S. (1993). *Education as adventure: Lessons from second grade.* New York: Teachers College Press.

Paley, V. (1993). *You can't say you can't play.* Cambridge, MA: Harvard University Press.

Pianta, R. (1999). *Enhancing relationships between children and teachers.* Washington, DC: American Psychological Association.

Stipek, D. (1998). *Motivation to learn: From theory to practice.* Needham Heights, MA: Prentice Hall.

TIPS FOR TEACHERS

Practicing teachers may want to adapt some of the observation and interview strategies for routine use in their classrooms. For example, teachers may elicit self-descriptions from their students (Strategies 5.2, 5.3) verbally or in writing as a way to get to know individuals at the beginning of the school year; it may be interesting to repeat this activity at the end of the year to document student growth.

Interview questions in Strategies 5.1 and 5.8 can be used in small group discussions as part of an elementary social skills curriculum to provide insights into students' social understandings and as a basis for further instructional activities. Teachers may use Strategy 5.10 to monitor actual social interactions of students.

Several strategies can be adapted for use as self-evaluation tools for professional development purposes. For example, to evaluate their own instructional practices and monitor interactions with different students, teachers may want to request that a colleague, mentor, or assistant utilize Strategies 5.7 and 5.14 with their students and provide feedback. Teachers can monitor student engagement in instructional activities on their own by utilizing Strategy 5.13. Teachers also may request assistance to find out how students view teacher qualities (Strategy 5.5) and their schoolwork (Strategy 5.12), or may address such questions themselves by asking older children to respond in writing and younger children to respond verbally in small discussion groups. Tools such as these are used in professional development programs to enhance understanding of student perspectives critical for their motivation to learn in school (e.g., McCombs & Whisler, 1997).

REFERENCES

Asher, S., and Dodge, K. (1986). Identifying children who are rejected by their peers. *Developmental Psychology, 22,* 444–449.

Babad, E., Bernieri, F., and Rosenthal, R. (1991). Students as judges of teachers' verbal and nonverbal behavior. *American Educational Research Journal, 28*, 211–234.

Berndt, T. (1981). Relations between social cognition, nonsocial cognition, and social behavior. In J. Flavel and L. Ross (Eds.), *Social cognitive development* (pp. 176–199). New York: Cambridge University Press.

Berndt, T. (1983). Social cognition, social behavior, and children's friendships: In E. Higgins, D. Ruble, and W. Hautup (Eds.). *Social cognition and social development: A sociocultural perspective* (pp. 158–192). New York: Cambridge University Press.

Berndt, T., and Keefe, K. (1992). Friends' influence on adolescents' perceptions of themselves at school. In D. Schunk and J. Meece (Eds.), *Student perceptions in the classroom* (pp. 51–73). Hillsdale, NJ: Erlbaum.

Birch, S., and Ladd, G. (1997). The teacher–child relationship and children's early school adjustment. *Journal of School Psychology, 35*, 61–79.

Bronfenbrenner, U. (1979). *The ecology of human development.* Cambridge, MA: Harvard University Press.

Bronfenbrenner, U., and Morris, P. (1998). The ecology of developmental processes. In W. Damon (Series Ed.) and R. Lerner (Vol. Ed.), *Handbook of child psychology, Vol. 1: Theoretical Models of Human Development* (5th ed., pp. 993–1027). New York: Wiley.

Bugental, J., and Zelen, S. (1950). Investigations into the self-concept: The W-A-Y technique. *Journal of Personality, 18*, 483–498.

Buhrmester, D., and Furman, W. (1986). The changing functions of friends in childhood: A new-Sullivanian perspective. In V. Derlega and B. Winstead (Eds.), *Friendship and social interaction.* New York: Springer Verlag.

Cassidy, J., Parke, R., Butkovsky, L., and Braungart, J. (1992). Family-peer connections. The roles of emotional expressiveness within the family and children's understanding of emotions. *Child Development, 63*, 603–618.

Coie, J., and Dodge, K. (1998). Aggression and antisocial behavior. In W. Damon (Series Ed.) and N. Eisenberg (Vol. Ed.), *Handbook of child psychology, Vol. 3: Social, emotional, and personality development* (5th ed., pp. 779–862). New York: Wiley.

Coie, J., Dodge, K., and Coppotelli, H. (1982). Dimensions of types of social status: A cross-age perspective. *Developmental Psychology, 18*, 557–560.

Csikszentmihalyi, M. (1990). *Flow: The psychology of optimal experience.* New York: Harper and Row.

Damon, W. (1984). Peer education: The untapped potential. *Journal of Applied Developmental Psychology, 5*, 331–343.

Damon, W., and Hart, D. (1982). The development of self-understanding from infancy through adolescence. *Child Development, 53*, 841–864.

Damon, W., and Hart, D. (1988). *Self-understanding in childhood and adolescence.* New York: Cambridge University Press.

Daniels, D., Kalkman, D., and McCombs, B. (2001). Young children's perspectives on learning and teacher practices in different classroom contexts: Implications for motivation. *Early Education and Development, 12*, 253–273.

Deci, E., and Ryan, R. (1985). *Intrinsic motivation and self-determination in human behavior.* New York: Plenum Press.

Dweck, C. (1999). *Self-theories: Their role in motivation, personality, and development.* Philadelphia, PA: Psychological Press.

Dweck, C., and Leggett, E. (1988). A social cognitive approach to motivation and personality. *Psychological Review, 95*, 256–273.

Eccles, J., Wigfield, A., and Schiefele, U. (1998). Motivation to succeed. In W. Damon (Series Ed.) and N. Eisenberg (Vol. Ed.), *Handbook of child psychology, Vol. 3: Social, emotional, and personality development* (5th ed., pp. 1017–1095). New York: Wiley.

Erdley, C., and Dweck, C. (1993). Children's implicit personality theories as predictors of their social judgments. *Child Development, 64*, 863–878.

Erikson, E. (1950). *Childhood and society.* New York: Norton.

Finn, J. (1989). Withdrawing from school. *Review of Educational Research, 59*, 117–142.

Finn, J., and Rock, D. (1997). Academic success among students at-risk. *Journal of Applied Psychology, 82*, 221–234.

Gnepp, J., and Chilamkurti, C. (1988). Children's use of personality attributions to predict other peoples' emotional and behavioral reactions. *Child Development, 59*, 743–754.

Goodenow, C. (1993). Classroom belonging among early adolescent students: Relationships to motivation and achievement. *Journal of Early Adolescence, 13*, 21–43.

Harris, P. (1989). *Children and emotion: The development of psychological understanding.* Oxford: Blackwell.

Harter, S. (1983). Developmental perspective on the self-system. In P. Mussen (Ed.), *Handbook of child psychology* (Vol. 4, pp. 275–385). New York: Wiley.

Harter, S. (1998). The development of self-representations. In W. Damon (Series Ed.) and N. Eisenberg (Vol. Ed.), *Handbook of child psychology, Vol. 3: Social, emotional, and personality development* (5th ed., pp. 553–617). New York: Wiley.

Harter, S., and Monsour, A. (1992). Developmental analysis of conflict caused by opposing attributes in the adolescent self-portrait. *Developmental Psychology, 28*, 251–260.

Harter, S., and Whitesell, N. (1989). Developmental changes in children's understanding of single, multiple, and blended emotion concepts. In C. Saarni and P. Harris (Ed.), *Children's understandings of emotions* (pp. 81–116). New York: Cambridge University Press.

Heller, K., and Berndt, T. (1981). Developmental changes in the formation and organization of personality attributions. *Child Development, 52*, 683–691.

Irwin, D. M., and Bushnell, M. M. (1980). *Observational strategies for child study.* New York: Harcourt Brace Jovanovich College Publishers.

Izard, C. (1972). *The face of emotion.* New York: Appleton-Century-Crofts.

Ladd, G. (1990). Having friends, keeping friends, making friends, and being liked by peers in the classroom: Predictors of children's early school adjustment? *Child Development, 61*, 1081–1100.

Ladd, G. (1996). Shifting ecologies during the 5 to 7 year period: Predicting children's adjustment during the transition to grade school. In A. Sameroff and M. Haith (Eds.), *The five to seven year shift: The age of reason and responsibility.* (pp. 363–386) Chicago, IL: University of Chicago Press.

Marks, H. (2000). Student engagement in instructional activity: Patterns in the elementary, middle, and high school years. *American Educational Research Journal, 37*, 153–184.

McCombs, B., and Whisler, J. (1997). *The learner-centered classroom and school: Strategies for increasing student motivation and achievement.* San Francisco: Jossey-Bass.

Midgley, C., Feldlaufer, H., and Eccles, J. (1989). Student/teacher relations and attitudes toward mathematics before and after the transition to junior high school. *Child Development, 60,* 981–992.

Montemayor, R., and Eisen, M. (1977). The development of self-conceptions from childhood to adolescence. *Developmental Psychology, 13,* 314–319.

Nicholls, J. (1978). The development of the concepts of effort and ability, perception of own attainment, and the understanding that difficult tasks require more ability. *Child Development, 49,* 811–814.

Odom, R., and Lemond, C. (1972). Developmental differences in the perception and production of facial expressions. *Child Development, 43,* 359–369.

Parten, M. (1932). Social participation among preschool children. *Journal of Abnormal and Social Psychology, 27,* 243–269.

Perry, K., and Weinstein, R. (1998). The social context of early schooling and children's school adjustment. *Educational Psychologist, 33,* 177–194.

Pianta, R. (1999). *Enhancing relationships between child and teachers.* Washington, DC: American Psychological Association.

Pianta, R., and Steinberg, M. (1992). Teacher–child relationships and the process of adjusting to school. In W. Damon (Series Ed.) and R. Pianta (Vol. Ed.), *New directions for child development: Beyond the parent: The roles of other adults in children's lives* (Vol. 57, pp. 61–79). San Francisoco: Jossey-Bass.

Renninger, K. A. (1998). Developmental psychology and instruction: Issues from and for practice. In W. Damon (Series Ed.) and I. Sigel and K. A. Renninger (Vol. Eds.), *Handbook of child psychology: Vol. 4: Child psychology in practice* (5th ed., pp. 211–274). New York: Wiley.

Rholes, W., Newman, L., and Ruble, D. (1990). Understanding self and other: Developmental and motivational aspects of perceiving persons in terms of invariant dispositions. In E. Higgins and R. Sorrentino (Eds.), *Handbook of motivation and cognition: Foundations of social behavior* (Vol 2., pp. 369–407). New York: Guilford Press.

Rubin, K., Bukowski, W., and Parker, J. (1998). Peer interactions, relationships, and groups. In W. Damon (Series Ed.) and N. Eisenberg (Vol. Ed.), *Handbook of child psychology, Vol. 3: Social, emotional, and personality development* (5th ed., pp. 619–700). New York: Wiley.

Rubin, K., and Coplan, R. (1992). Peer relations in childhood. *Developmental psychology: An advanced textbook* (pp. 519–577). Hillsdale, NJ: Erlbaum.

Ruble, D., and Dweck, C. (1995). The development of self-conceptions and person conceptions. In N. Eisenberg (Ed.) *Review of personality and social psychology* (Vol. 15) (pp. 109–139). Thousand Oaks, CA: Sage.

Ruble, D. (1983). The development of social comparison processes and their role in achievement-related self-socialization. In T. Higgins, D. Ruble, and W. Hartup (Eds.), *Social cognition and social development: A sociocultural perspective* (pp. 134–157) New York: Cambridge University Press.

Ryan, R., and Stiller, J. (1991). The social contexts of internalization: Parent and teacher influences on autonomy, motivation, and learning. In P. Pintrich and M. Maehr

(Eds.), *Advances in motivation and Achievement: Goals and self-regulatory processes* (Vol. 7, pp. 115–149). Greenwich, CT: JAI.

Saarni, C., Mumme, D., and Campos, J. (1998). Emotional development: Action, communication, and understanding. In W. Damon (Series Ed.) and N. Eisenberg (Vol. Ed.), *Handbook of child psychology, Vol. 3: Social, emotional, and personality development* (5th ed., pp. 237–309). New York: Wiley.

Savin-Williams, R., and Berndt, T. (1990). Friendships and peer relations during adolescense. In S. Feldman and G. Elliott (ed.), *At the threshold: The developing adolescent* (pp. 277–307). Cambridge, MA: Harvard University Press.

Selman, R. (1981). What children understand of intrapsychic processes: The child as a budding personality theorist. In E. Shapiro and E. Weber (Eds.), *Cognitive and affective growth: Developmental interaction* (pp. 187–215). Hillsdale, NJ: Erlbaum.

Skinner, E., and Belmont, M. (1993). Motivation in the classroom: Reciprocal effects of teacher behavior and student engagement across the school year. *Journal of Educational Psychology, 85*, 571–581.

Stipek, D. (1981). Children's perceptions of their own and their classmates' ability. *Journal of Educational Psychology, 73*, 404–410.

Stipek, D., Feiler, R., Byler, P., Ryan, R., Milburn, S., and Salmon, J. (1998). Good beginnings: What difference does the program make in preparing young children for school? *Journal of Applied Developmental Psychology, 19*, 41–66.

Stipek, D. (1998). *Motivation to Learn: From Theory to Practice,* 3rd ed. Needham Heights, MA: Allyn & Bacon.

Stipek, D., and Daniels, D. (1988). Declining perceptions of competence: A consequence of changes in the child or in the educational environment? *Journal of Educational Psychology, 80*, 352–356.

Stipek, D., and Daniels, D. (1990). Children's use of dispositional attributions in predicting the performance and behavior of classmates. *Journal of Applied Developmental Psychology, 11*, 13–28.

Stipek, D., Feiler, R., Daniels, D., and Milburn, S. (1995). Effects of different instructional approaches on young children' achievement and motivation. *Child Development, 66*, 209–223.

Stipek, D., and MacIver, D. (1989). Developmental change in children's assessment of intellectual competence. *Child Development, 60*, 521–538.

Strayer, J. (1986). Children's attributions regarding the situational determinents of emotions in self and others. *Developmental Psychology, 17*, 649–654.

Sullivan, H. S. (1953). *The interpersonal theory of psychiatry.* New York: Norton.

Weiner, B. (1985). An attributional theory of achievement motivation and emotion. *Psychological Review, 92*, 548–573.

Weinstein, R. (1983). Student perceptions of schooling. *The Elementary School Journal, 83*, 289–312.

Wentzel, K. (1997). Student motivation in middle school: The role of perceived pedagogical caring. *Journal of Educational Psychology, 89*, 411–419.

Wentzel, K., and Asher, S. (1995). The academic lives of neglected, rejected, popular, and controversial children. *Child Development, 66*, 754–763.

White, K., and Jones, K. (in press). Effects of teacher feedback on the reputations and peer perceptions of children with behavior problems. *Journal of Experimental Child Psychology.*

White, K., and Kistner, J. (1992). The influence of teacher feedback on young children's peer preferences and perceptions. *Developmental Psychology, 28,* 933–940.

Yussen, S., and Kane, P. (1985). Children's conception of intelligence. In S. Yussen (Ed.), *The growth of reflection in children* (pp. 207–241). Orlando, FL: Academic Press.

Integrating Observations and Interviews: Child Profiles

CHAPTER PREVIEW

This chapter is intended to provide examples of how strategies from this guide can be used to construct a developmental profile of a child in school. The focus is to facilitate a more holistic understanding of an individual child's development and functioning in the school setting by the integration of physical, cognitive, and socioemotional information obtained through the interviews and observations.

INTEGRATING OBSERVATIONS AND INTERVIEWS

Observations and interviews can be incorporated to construct a cohesive profile of an individual child. The approach used in the creation of the following profile was to integrate physical, cognitive, and socioemotional data obtained from some strategies in this guide to provide a snapshot of the child's current level of development. Interpretations are based on comparison with similar-aged classmates and background knowledge of developmental theory and research. The observation strategies provide information about demonstrated skills, behaviors, and attitudes. The interview strategies provide information regarding a child's personal perspective or understanding of an experience. A deeper understanding of the child is gained through combining these approaches (see Chapter 2).

The two profile samples have integrated information from a large number of observations and interviews to obtain a fairly comprehensive description of the child across the physical, cognitive, and socioemotional domains. Students with limited observation and interview time may not be able to construct such detailed or complete descriptions, however they may be able to construct a brief portrait of a child focusing on one or two domains of development.

The profiles below were constructed by compiling notes across strategies. Strategies used (indicated by parentheses) are imbedded within the profile description. Figures illustrating completed data forms are included to demonstrate correspondence

123

between raw observations/interviews and child descriptions. A brief developmental analysis of each profile is provided in a summary, followed by reflections on the implications of the information for education.

CHILD PROFILES

Name: Susan

Grade: 2

Date: May 2001

Observations/Interviews Conducted: *February–April 2001*

Susan is an eight-year-old second grader. Susan's teacher reports that Susan has grown several inches during this school year but still remains shorter than most of the other children, both boys and girls, in her classroom. **(3.1)** Susan appears to weigh about the same as most of her classmates, making her slightly heavy for her height. Susan thinks her mom is pretty because of her long, dark hair and brown eyes. **(3.2)** Susan also thinks that she is "pretty" because she has long dark hair and brown eyes, "like my mom." **(5.2)** Note that Susan describes herself according to her physical attributes, a common tendency for a child her age.

Susan stated that she likes her teacher and that she feels that her teacher cares about her. **(5.6)** Susan appears to seek more attention from her teacher than do other children in the classroom. Susan looked at her teacher often while completing the writing assignment that was part of the daily classroom routine. She was observed to get out of her seat to talk to her teacher on three occasions within the first 10 minutes of the school day to talk about the weather or an after-school activity, and to give the teacher a pencil. **(5.7) (See Figure 6.1.)**

Susan says she likes school, especially reading class. **(5.12)** The classroom aide was seated next to Susan during reading class. Susan was often observed to ask the aide for help with her reading assignment. Observations of Susan's reading class reveal that Susan has difficulty paying attention and often loses her place when other children in the classroom are reading. **(5.13)** Susan looks at her teacher and seems to try to pay attention when her teacher talks, but she begins to fidget in her desk when the lesson requires concentration (i.e., finding answers to teacher questions in the text). It is unknown if Susan is weak in some reading strategies, is distracted, or is just uninterested in the story. Susan's teacher indicates that Susan's grades are pretty average. She indicates that Susan seems to prefer to be read to rather than to read, and that Susan does have some difficulty with decoding unfamiliar words. An observation of Susan and a classmate reading together demonstrated this. Susan read at an uneven pace, speeding up at some times and slowing down at others, occasionally stumbling over a word. Her reading partner waited patiently for Susan to correctly identify the word. Susan gave up quickly, identifying "caftan" as "cattail." Her reading partner did not immediately tell her the correct word, but told her to "try it again, and look at the middle letters and ending." **(adapted 4.2)** Susan responded well to the direction, but did not demonstrate any reciprocal guidance toward her partner. Susan was the weaker reader of the two.

Susan's movement around the classroom is generally as coordinated and skillful as other children her age. In physical education class and on the playground Susan was observed to hop on one foot and appears to have mastered skipping. **(3.6)** Her fine motor skills also appear similar to others in her grade. Susan was asked to draw a picture of a cube from a model provided her. **(3.5)** **(see Figure 6.2.)** Her figure shows an early understanding of the relation among parts that is expected for a child her age. Susan signed her picture by printing her name. The letters are all formed correctly and printed evenly. Susan stated that she is beginning to learn to write in cursive, but it "isn't as neat."

Susan was observed while on the playground during recess. She was sitting with two other girls on a concrete stoop, coloring pictures in a book. **(3.8)** Susan and her friends can be described as "prosocial" playmates. According to Susan, "we don't fight because we like to play the same things." **(5.8)** While Susan and her friends were "playing school," one of Susan's playmates was overheard to say, "I'll be the teacher, and you two are the kids." Perspective-taking appears to be developing in Susan. She is beginning to develop the ability to see the situation from someone else's viewpoint (i.e., "we take turns being the teacher because everyone likes that role"). **(4.1)**

The girls were not very active on the playground, preferring to sit and color pictures. When asked what they were coloring Susan responded, "All of us have animal coloring books, but mine is the only one with dolphins in it. I wanted a book of water animals. There are also pictures of sea turtles in here." Susan's response provided some evidence of her ability to classify objects. Her ability was again demonstrated on another occasion when she was given a group of animal pictures and asked to put them in some kind of order. **(4.5)** Susan separated the animals into water, land, and air groups. **(See Figure 6.3.)**

Susan is a generally healthy child and seemed happy on the occasions she was observed. According to Susan's teacher, Susan's only absences this year have been due to a short illness with the flu. Susan complained on several occasions during her class's standardized testing that her stomach hurt. However, she was able to complete the testing without having to leave the classroom. The school nurse indicates that it is not uncommon for children of Susan's age to complain of physical ailments when they do not like or are anxious about their school work. **(3.9)**

Figure 6.1

Strategy 5.7: Observations of Teacher-Student Interactions Record Form for Susan, a second grader.

Sample Record of One Event

Target Child ___Susan___

Event #1:   Setting ___Classroom___   Date _3/25_ Time _8:30_

Initiator: Teacher _____ Child _✓_

Bid: Touch ____ Name ____ Talk _✓_ Position _✓_

Request ____ Demand ____ Disrupt ____ Other _____

Brief Description: _waits to give teacher pencil S. found on floor. Tells her she found it by her desk._

Response: Immediate _✓_ Delay ____ time: ____ Ignore _____

Affect: Positive _✓_ Neutral ____ Negative _____

Brief Description: _Thanks S. Redirects her to task._

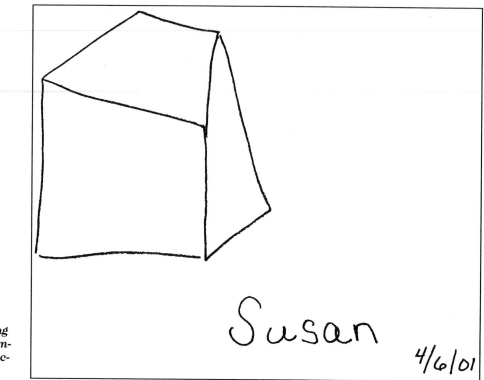

Figure 6.2.

Strategy 3.5: Drawing and handwriting sample from Susan, a second grader.

Task 4: Classifying Animal Pictures

Child: Susan

Date: March 25, 2001

Susan classified animal pictures according to whether they were usually found on land, in water, or in the air.

Land	Water	Air
bear	shark	bee
collie	lobster	robin
mouse	pelican (mistake)	fly
monkey	whale	hummingbird
cat	dolphin	
	fish	

Figure 6.3.

Strategy 6.5: Example of Susan's responses for Classes and Relations tasks.

Reflection and Interpretation Susan is one of the shortest children in her second grade classroom. However, Susan's physical growth appears to be within a developmentally appropriate range. Her motor skill development further supports this conclusion. Susan's attitude regarding her appearance is positive and she seems to have a healthy self-concept. Susan demonstrates some concrete operational thinking skill as is appropriate for her age. Susan shows some "neediness" by her attention-seeking behavior with her teacher and the classroom aide, but she demonstrates skill and confidence in her interactions with her classmates.

Implications for Education Some suggestions for helping Susan at school can be gained from reviewing her profile. Susan may need encouragement to participate in more physically active behaviors in order to increase her exercise. Although Susan's weight is not of concern to her at this time, it may become a concern as she matures and enters adolescence. Susan's teachers can help her to maintain her positive self-concept and to be happy with herself by providing encouragement when she participates in physically active behaviors (e.g., playground games, athletics) and challenging academic tasks.

Susan's teacher also may use her positive relationship with Susan to encourage her to work more independently. Susan's "need for reassurance" can be addressed with patience and through positive reinforcement of "appropriate" use of time. Susan's teacher also can use information about her interests and strengths from interviews and observations to encourage and motivate Susan.

Name: José

Grade: 5

Date: April 2001

Observations/Interviews Conducted: January — April 2001

José is a dark-haired, medium-sized boy in fifth grade; he just turned 11. As compared to the other boys in the fifth grade class, he is of average height, up to a head taller than some and a head shorter than others. **(3.1)** He is showing some subtle signs of puberty: a glistening face and a few pimples sprinkled across his nose. He appears to reflect on his appearance, making comments on his new "buzz" cut and "cool" baggy shorts, as well as the fact that he is "right in the middle" of the boys with regard to height. **(3.2)** He claims that it doesn't matter how tall he is, that he learned in health class that "how tall kids are now doesn't show how tall they will be when they are grown."

Although he is mostly attentive and does his work on his own in class **(5.13)**, José often fidgets about in his seat **(3.3)**, looking at the clock from time to time, especially before lunch or recess. To him, a good school day is when they have gym and longer recesses. He likes to play sports games on the playground, "nothing else." **(3.4)** He doesn't like some rules, such as the one stating that they can only play touch-football, claiming that it isn't "real" football. He suggests that the teacher should only make those rules if someone really gets hurt playing tackle. Observations of his behavior on the playground support his stated interests. **(3.8)** On two different occasions, he was seen engaged in sports activities (e.g., football, basketball) with a large group of boys. **(See Figure 6.4.)** With regard to his gross motor skills, he demonstrated accurate throwing and catching during these activities, maneuvering his body gracefully. **(3.6)** However, at other times he demonstrated some awkwardness in running. On another occasion, a hot day with few active games occurring, he was seen sitting up high on the jungle gym watching the surrounding activities. This playground has only a few, small cool areas for play on hot days (the trees are small and provide little shade); children spend more time "hanging out" and socializing in smaller groups **(5.10)** and less in organized sports play on these days; there is little else to do.

José was seen coming from the nurse's office with a band-aid on his elbow one day after lunch recess. The school nurse had remarked that children often came in from recess for band-aids. There was often very little blood, she suspected that most just wanted "a comforting smile and a little attention," **(3.9)** and were happy to return to the playground after a minute or two. She said that children often come to her office with stomachaches for the same reason; she calls their parents if the ache persists. The nurse commented that she feels sorry for children when their parents can not be reached quickly, because she often has to leave them in the office when she has to go to another school.

José's fine motor skills were observed during several classroom activities. **(3.5)** Interestingly, José showed deliberate, refined cursive writing at times (spelling tests and essays) and quick, messy writing using large letters at other times (writing in assignment notebook). In art class, he demonstrated deliberate attention to detail and perspective in a complex drawing of a castle with a moat surrounding it.

Evidence of José's cognitive skills (e.g., problem solving, perspective-taking) was gathered from several different observations of classroom behavior as well as from his responses to brief interviews and staged tasks. For example, José's focused attention, planning, and perspective-taking abilities were observed while he played a board game with a few classmates during a free activity time in the classroom. **(4.1)** He was clearly absorbed in the game, giving it his full attention (appeared not to notice the noise in the classroom). He demonstrated understanding of the objective of the game as well as many complex rules. This was indicated when José explained the rules to one boy who was less familiar with the game. José appeared to take this boy's experience into account, as he would frequently make statements like "you know how when we played…" or "this is kind of like…" in his explanations of the rules and received an "oh, yeah" in response. Once when he did not receive a response (the boy looked puzzled), he said, "look, I'll show you…. See?" and waited for a reply. He also showed some advanced planning in making his own moves as well as in explaining them to others (similar to how he stopped to think before attempting mazes). **(4.11)** It appeared as if the explanations were sufficient to involve all the boys in the game (although this observer was not entirely clear about the objective and strategies based on the brief explanations).

José's ability to consider another's perspective, at least to some extent, was also demonstrated in his response to Holly's dilemma. **(4.3)** He not only showed evidence of his ability to take the perspective of each major player (one at a time), but some evidence of coordinating two perspectives ("an outsider's perspective") and sympathizing with the players involved.

José demonstrated fairly sophisticated classification skills in his sorting of baseball cards in a hierarchy; he could also easily suggest other ways to categorize the cards (e.g., by popularity, monetary worth, position). **(4.5)** He enjoys classifying and reclassifying his many Pokemon cards as well.

José reports liking math in school, and being good at it. **(5.3, 5.12)** He demonstrated efficient retrieval of simple addition and subtraction solutions in a timed review test, stating that this was "easy, I knew this in first grade." He likes the word problems and geometry work they're doing in class now.

He reports liking to read at home and some novels at school, but claims that language arts and English are not his favorite subjects. **(5.12)** He states that writing essays is "hard" for him and that he doesn't like "answering questions about stories" or other reading materials ("especially in social studies, it's boring"). José's grades are consistent with his interests and stated competencies; he consistently receives A's in Math and B's in Language Arts.

José is a fluent reader, and appears to think about meaning while he reads. When reading a passage from a Harry Potter book aloud, he stopped to clarify the meaning of a phrase he was unfamiliar with, and seemed relieved when he "got it." **(4.8)** He also chooses to read the Harry Potter series (for the second time) during free reading time in the classroom; several other students are also re-reading the series. Occasionally the children chuckle to themselves or whisper a phrase or incident to a classmate. One phrase from the book shared among the boys is a derogatory comment about a character (e.g., "Dudley is like a young killer whale"), perhaps demonstrating the children's beginning understandings of metaphor. **(4.9)**

Although the class schedule varies (especially during "theme week"), José spends most of his time in school doing independent seatwork and in whole class instructional activities. **(4.12)** He participates in whole class discussion by raising his hand to respond to their teacher's questions (his responses are usually appropriate). **(5.7)** His teacher appears to have noticed José's timidity in participating in small group work and tries to get him to participate more actively with groups in other settings. **(5.10)** The teacher responds to José warmly and with praise when he does participate. Joey's abilities to help classmates may also be aided by other social cognitive abilities, such as his abilities to distinguish and explain emotions and dispositions. **(5.1, 5.4)** José sees himself as pretty smart, helpful, and shy. He discriminates between what he is good at and not good at (e.g., especially sports that take advantage of his skills). **(5.3)**

José feels that he has friends and is accepted at school by teachers and classmates alike. **(5.6, 5.11)** He describes friends as those who get along and like to do the "same kinds of stuff, I like to do." **(5.8)** José does not think he is popular (e.g., "I didn't get picked for student council") however he thinks he is more popular than some other students who get picked on ("He always gets blamed and he didn't even do anything"). **(5.9)**

	José Child 1	Mary Child 2	Paul Child 3	Jim Child 4
Age group: 11-12				
Observation: ① 2 3 4 5				
Date: 4/20/01				
Gender:	Ⓜ F	M Ⓕ	Ⓜ F	Ⓜ F
Size of group (#)	10	3	1	10
Physical level of behavior				
Active Play				
Vigorous	✓			✓
Rough and Tumble				
Games with rules	✓			✓
Passive Play				
Talking		✓		
Walking				
Sitting				
Waiting			✓	
Solitary Active Play				
Solitary Passive Play				
Play w/same gender peer(s)	✓	✓		✓
Play w/opposite gender peer(s)				
Location of child				
Swing area				
Slides				
Jungle gym				
Hard surface area	✓	✓		✓
Grass/field area				
Other (describe)			✓ Beside Bldg.	
Adult directed attention				
Observer directed attention				
	Basketball	Conversation	Timed out	Basketball

Figure 6.4

Straegy 3.8: Observations of Playground Behavior Record Form for José, a fifth grader.

Figure 6.5

Example of Strategy 5.5: Teacher Qualities Response for José, a fifth grader

		Caring		Responsive		Interesting		Ind Inst.		Fair		Personal		Manager		Other	
		+	-	+	-	+	-	+	-	+	-	+	-	+	-	+	-
José	Child 1		−	+			—		−		−	+		+				
Jim	Child 2		−	+			—		−	+		+		+				
Jeff	Child 3	+		+			—		−		−		+		−			

José describes a good teacher as one who provides interesting schoolwork; he hates doing the same thing over again and thinks that he should be able to "choose what to do sometimes." **(5.12)** Observations of his classroom indicate that José's concerns about having little choice, and doing lots of repetitive seatwork are warranted. **(5.14)** He also proposed that good teachers care about how well he does ("like my piano teacher...she cares if I don't play a note right"). **(5.5)** **(See Figure 6.5.)**

Reflection and Interpretation Typical of a child entering early adolescence Joey demonstrates some unevenness of development. He demonstrates abilities to engage in abstract thinking and complex problem-solving in some domains. His social understandings and skills appear exemplary in some contexts, and somewhat less developed than his peers in others. Joey's concerns and interests appear typical of a boy his age.

Implications for Education Several ideas for enhancing Joey's education and development can be gleaned from this profile. It appears as if Joey is ready for some academic challenges, and could use his developing cognitive and social skills in conducting authentic learning projects with peers in small groups. Such experiences may also foster his self-confidence and engagement in school, as such projects allowing for more social interaction and physical activity. Joey also needs to be prepared for the transition to middle school; perhaps his teacher can talk with him and his parents about concerns, expectations, and special preparations.

Joey's teacher may be able to benefit from reflecting on Joey's feelings and perspectives, especially his concerns with lacking choice in the classroom. The teacher has the opportunity to use this information to determine options for improving instruction and enhancing student motivation.

CHAPTER SUMMARY

The child profiles provided in this chapter demonstrate how observations and interviews can enable educators to better understand children's perspectives, learning, and development essential for their success in the classroom. Developmental and educational psychologists stress the importance of "listening" to children and of becoming "sensitive" to their understanding of the world (see Chapter 1). Educators are able to convey their interests in and support of children when they are attuned to their perspectives.

Sample Parent Information Letter

Date:

Dear Parent or Guardian:

My name is _____ and I am a student at _____, currently enrolled in a course on child development. To fulfill the requirements of the course, I will be observing children at _____School this semester. I will observe

children in different settings (e.g., classrooms, playground) on several occasions, and write notes about their behavior. The purpose of this class assignment is to enhance my understanding of children's perspectives, learning, and behavior at different ages. I will not identify children or use their names in any notes or class assignments submitted to the instructor.

If you have any questions about this class project, please contact my course instructor, _____at _____.

Sincerely,

_____

Student's Signature

Sample Parent Consent Form

Date:

Dear Parent or Guardian:

My name is _____ and I am a student at _____.

I am currently enrolled in a course on child development and behavior. As part of the requirements for this course, I am conducting brief studies of children in their schools. The purpose of this class assignment is to enhance my understanding of everyday behavior and thinking of children at different grade levels.

Therefore, I would like to request permission to study your child. The study may involve several brief interviews (10–15 minutes), participation in simple games or tasks (e.g., puzzles, card games), and behavioral observations at school. No formal or standardized tests or assessments (e.g., school achievement tests, personality or intelligence tests) will be administered.

Your child's participation is entirely voluntary, and he or she may withdraw from participating at any time.

Confidentiality of your child's responses will be protected. She or he will be identified by a false name in class assignments submitted to my course instructor.

If you have any questions about this class project, please contact my course instructor, _____, at _____.

Sincerely,

_____

I _____, give permission for my child, _____ to participate in a child study project being conducted by _____
for a course in child development and behavior. I have read the above letter and understand its contents.

_____   _____
Signature   Date

Record Forms

Record Form 3.1: Observations of Body Growth and Physical Development

Age Group: _____

	Child 1	Child 2	Child 3	Child 4	Child 5
Gender:	M F	M F	M F	M F	M F

Mark an X on the line corresponding to the observed height, weight, and race.

Height:
    Below Ave.   _____   _____   _____   _____   _____
    Average   _____   _____   _____   _____   _____
    Above Ave.   _____   _____   _____   _____   _____

Weight:
    Below Ave.   _____   _____   _____   _____   _____
    Average   _____   _____   _____   _____   _____
    Above Ave.   _____   _____   _____   _____   _____

Ethnicity:
    Caucasian   _____   _____   _____   _____   _____
    African Amer.   _____   _____   _____   _____   _____
    Hispanic   _____   _____   _____   _____   _____
    Asian   _____   _____   _____   _____   _____
    Other   _____   _____   _____   _____   _____

Body Shape Codes: (Meso, Ecto, Endo)
Body Shape: _____   _____   _____   _____   _____

Indications of Puberty: Adolescent Growth Spurt
     Y N   Y N   Y N   Y N   Y N

Other Indicators of Puberty (list):
   _____   _____   _____   _____   _____

Record Form 3.2: Children's Perceptions of Attractiveness Response Sheet

Age: _____

1. Tell me about what you think makes a person look good (attractive).

Girl 1:

Girl 2:

Boy 1:

Boy 2:

2. Who do you think looks good (attractive)?

Girl 1:

Girl 2:

Boy 1:

Boy 2:

3. Do you think other people have different ideas about what makes a person look good (attractive)? If so, tell me about what they might think.

Girl 1:

Girl 2:

Boy 1:

Boy 2:

Record Form 3.3: Observation of School Day Activity

Grades K–8

Observation of School Day Activity

Grade _____

Observation Time _____

	Child 1 — Gender M/F			**Child 2 — Gender M/F**	
Time begin	Time end	Activity	Time begin	Time end	Activity

Record Form 3.4: Preferred Physical Activities Response Sheet

Age level: _____

Classroom Free-Time Activities

1. What are some things you like to do in your classroom when you have free time? Tell me about them.

   Probes: When you do them?

   Who you do them with?

   What are the rules?

2. What are some things your friends like to do during free time in the classroom? Tell me about them.

   Probes: What are some of the different kinds of activities your friends like to do? Do your friends like to do the same kinds of things that you do?

Playground Activities

3. What kinds of activities (games, behaviors) do you like to do on the playground?

   Probes: Tell me about your favorite place to play.

4. Tell me about what you like most about the playground. Why? Who do you play with?

5. Tell me about your playmates on the playground.

   Probes: Only boys or girls or both? Why?

6. Tell me about what your friends like to do on the playground.

   A. What do you do if everyone doesn't want to play the same thing?

7. Tell me about the playground rules.

   Probe: How do the rules affect your play?

8. Tell me about what you would change on the playground.

   Probe: Why is that?

Physical Education Class

9. Tell what you do in physical education class.

   Probes: Tell me about how much time you spend doing each thing. Do you do the same thing each class?

(continued on following page)

(continued from previous page)

10. Tell me about what you like best in physical education class?
    Probes: Tell me more about that.

    Tell me more about why you like it.

    How is it played?

    How many can be involved?

    Is it more fun with more or fewer players?

    Tell me about how much skill you need.

11. Tell me about what you like least to do in physical education class.
    Probes: Why does the teacher have you do those things?

Record Form 3.5: Drawing and Handwriting Skills Checklist

Age of Child_____
Gender of Child _____

Drawing Skills (check the classification that best describes the drawing of the cube):

1. _____   Scribble

2. _____   Single Unit

3. _____   Differentiated Figure

4. _____   Integrated Whole

Handwriting Skills (check all that apply):

1. _____   Name printed

2. _____   Name printed mostly in upper case letters

3. _____   Some letter reversals

4. _____   Name written in cursive

5. _____   All letters formed correctly

6. _____   Letters uneven size or height

7. _____   Letters too thin or too round

8. _____   Letters written too light or too heavy

9. _____   Letters written shaky or broken

10. _____   Letters uniform size

Record Form 3.6: Gross Motor Skill Checklist

Age: _____

	Child 1				Child 2			
	M F				M F			
	Observe	Not observe	Success	Not success	Observe	Not observe	Success	Not success
Locomotion								
Hop on one foot								
Able to skip smoothly								
Walk/run smoothly								
Manipulation								
Accurately throw large ball								
Accurately throw small ball								
Catch ball								
Accurately roll ball								
Accurately kick ball								
Stability/Balance								
Balance on one leg								
Walk on balance-type beam								
Dodge ball without falling								
Carry w/out spilling/ dropping								
Body Awareness								
Avoid bumping other children								
Avoid objects when moving in class								
Comfortable talking distance								

Record Form 3.7: Playground Environment Checklist/Rating Scale

Section I. Play Areas

1. _____ A hard surface area with space for games.

2. _____ Play equipment available (i.e., Balls, jump ropes, bases, etc.)

3. _____ Equipment for active play

   _____ Slide(s)

   _____ Swing(s)

   _____ Climbing structure(s)

4. _____ Ample space for various types of large-muscle exercise & movement

5. _____ Equipment to encourage balance, coordination, and strength (i.e., Low Balance beam, chinning bars, etc.

6. _____ Grass area for chasing or organized games

7. _____ Sand play area and equipment to support sand play

8. _____ Water play area and equipment to support water play

9. _____ Structures for creative play (house, boat, car, etc.)

10. _____ Stage area for dramatic play

11. _____ Natural area that can attract birds, butterflies, bugs, etc.

12. _____ Garden area and tools

13. _____ Shade areas

14. _____ Area with tables/benches

15. _____ Area for social interaction with peers

Section II. Playground Safety

1. _____ Protective fence separating hazardous areas

2. _____ Shock-absorbing surfacing material under all climbing and moving equipment (e.g., sand, wood chips, shredded tire, etc.)

3. _____ Equipment matched to size of children (i.e., small equipment for younger, smaller students, etc.)

4. _____ Play area clean and free of litter, broken glass, etc.

5. _____ Equipment free of sharp edges, with no broken parts, in good repair

6. _____ Children within eyesight of playground monitors

(continued on following page)

(continued from previous page)

Section III. Type of Play Opportunities

(In other words, what can you expect to see children doing on this playground?)

1. _____   Encourages play; is inviting with easy access

2. _____   Promotes creativity with versatile equipment

3. _____   Encourages socializing

4. _____   Provides graduated challenges to foster physical development (e.g., obstacle course, chin-up bars, balance bar, etc.)

5. _____   Promotes various types of play (i.e., functional, constructive, dramatic, organized with rules)

6. _____   Equipment is movable to conform to children's creative play

7. _____   Playground is accessible for children with disabilities

Section IV. Complexity of Playground Equipment

Rate the complexity of the playground equipment on the scale following the item by circling the number that best describes the complexity of the equipment.

Swing(s)

(1) single swing set, simple sling- seat swing(s), all same size

(2) multiple swing sets, limited size variation

Slide(s)

(1) single slide, low height

(2) multiple slides, various heights

(3) multiple slides, various heights, widths, and shapes

Climbing structure(s)

(1) simple structure, one level, one climbing surface

(2) more complex structure, multiple levels OR more than one climbing surface

(3) most complex structure, multiple levels AND multiple climbing surfaces

Creative play structure(s)

(1) single play structure, one-dimensional play focus (e.g., row boat with seats)

(2) single play structure, multidimensional play focus (e.g., row boat with seats and bell)

(3) single or multiple play structures, with multidimensional play focus and multiple play areas (e.g., multiple deck ship, ladders between floors, seats, bell, steering wheel, slide off back)

(continued on following page)

(continued from previous page)

Section V. Playground Appeal

Circle the number that best describes the general appeal of the playground according to the following criteria.

Functionality of Playground Equipment (i.e., supports and encourages play and exercise)

(1) does not meet expected function

(2) meets expected function

(3) exceeds expected function

Comfort level of equipment and general area

(1) metal equipment, asphalt, limited space

(2) metal equipment, grass area

(3) non-metal equipment, grass area, tables/benches, shade

Aesthetic (visual appeal)

(1) drab, dull, uninteresting

(2) colorful, interesting

(3) bright, stimulating

Creative

(1) limited in type(s) of creative play encouraged

(2) encourages various types of creative play but opportunities limited to children at single age or level of motor skill development

(3) encourages various types of creative play in children at various ages and levels of motor skill development

Record Form 3.8: Observation of Playground Behaviors

Age group: _____

Observation: 1   2   3   4   5

Date: _____

	Child 1	Child 2	Child 3	Child 4
Gender:	M F	M F	M F	M F
Size of Group (#)	_____	_____	_____	_____
Physical Level of Behavior				
Active play				
Vigorous	_____	_____	_____	_____
Rough and tumble	_____	_____	_____	_____
Games with rules	_____	_____	_____	_____
Passive play				
Talking	_____	_____	_____	_____
Walking	_____	_____	_____	_____
Sitting	_____	_____	_____	_____
Waiting	_____	_____	_____	_____
Solitary active play	_____	_____	_____	_____
Solitary passive play	_____	_____	_____	_____
Play w/same gender peer(s)	_____	_____	_____	_____
Play w/opposite gender peer(s)	_____	_____	_____	_____
Location of child				
Swing area	_____	_____	_____	_____
Slides	_____	_____	_____	_____
Jungle gym	_____	_____	_____	_____
Hard surface area	_____	_____	_____	_____
Grass/field area	_____	_____	_____	_____
Other (describe)	_____	_____	_____	_____
Adult-directed attention	_____	_____	_____	_____
Observer-directed attention	_____	_____	_____	_____

Record Form 4.4: Conservation Tasks

	Prediction	Conclusion	Explanation	Conserver?
Child 1 Age ____				
Liquid				
Mass				
Number				
Child 2 Age ____				
Liquid				
Mass				
Number				

Record Form 4.7: Arithmetic Strategies Chart

	Guess	Show	Count from 1	Min	Decompose	Retrieve	Other
Pre-K							
Child 1							
Child 2							
Grades 1–2							
Child 1							
Child 2...							
Grade 3 and on							
Child 1							
Child 2...							

Record Form 4.8 (Part 2): Reading Skills and Strategies

	Visual Cues	Phonetic Cues	Automaticity	Fluency	Strategies (describe)	Other
Kindergarten						
Child 1						
Child 2...						
Grades 1–2						
Child 1						
Child 2...						
Grades 3–4						
Child 1						
Child 2...						
Grades 5–8						
Child 1						
Child 2...						

Record Form 4.11: Planning and Problem Solving

Age _____

Planning (before task)

     Time spent _____

     Child's behavior _____

     Child's explanation _____

Performance (during task)

     # of mistakes/wrong turns _____

     # of corrections _____

     Child's behavior/affect/spontaneous comments

Evaluation: Partial or elaborate planning

Record Form 4.12: Activity Setting Descriptions

Grade _____   **Time Observed: Morning   Afternoon**

Brief description of child and major activities involved in during observation period.

_____

_____

_____

	Small Group with Teacher	Small Group with Peers	Independent Centers	Whole Group	Seatwork Self	Other: Mentor or Tutor
Who?						
What?						
When?						
# Minutes						
Where?						
Why?						
Child's Participation Rating (1–5)						

Record Form 5.1: Identifying Facial Expressions and Emotions

	Happy	Sad	Fear	Anger	Disgust	Surprise	Interest	Shame
Total Child 1: Age _____								
Recognize Expression								
Label Expression								
Label Emotion								
Explain Cause								
Child 2: Age _____								
Recognize Expression								
Label Expression								
Label Emotion								
Explain Cause								
Child 3: Age _____								
Recognize Expression								
Label Expression								
Label Emotion								
Explain Cause								
Total Appropriate Responses:								

Record Form 5.2: Self-Descriptions

	Child Age 4–6	Child Age 7–9	Child Age 10–14
Gender			
Age			
Group Membership			
Preferences/Interests			
Activities			
Physical Characteristics			
Personality			
Competencies			
Interpersonal Character			
Beliefs, Values			
Other			

Record Form 5.4: Predicting Hypothetical Classmates' Behavior

	Smart			Not Smart			Nice			Not Nice		
	Academic	Social	Physical	Academic	Social	Physical	Academic	Social	Physical	Academic	Social	Physical
Child Age 5–6												
Child Age 7–8												
Child Age 9–10												
Child Age 11–14												

Record Form 5.5: Qualities of a Good Teacher

	Caring		Responsive		Interesting		Ind Inst.		Fair		Personal		Manager		Other	
	+	-	+	-	+	-	+	-	+	-	+	-	+	-	+	-
Child 1																
Child 2																
Child 3																

Record Form 5.7: Observations of Teacher-Student Interaction

Target Child _____

Event #1:   Setting_____   Date _____ Time _____

   Initiator: Teacher _____ Child _____

     Bid: Touch ____ Name _____ Talk _____ Position _____

      Request _____ Demand _____ Disrupt _____ Other _____

   Brief Description:

Response: Immediate _____ Delay _____ Time: ____ Ignore _____

     Affect: Positive _____ Neutral _____ Negative _____

   Brief Description:

Record Form 5.8: Children's Views of Friends

	Playmate	Companion	Reciprocal	Prosocial	Intimacy	Loyal	Support	Other
Child Age ____								
Child Age ____								
Child Age ____								

Record Form 5.10: Social Behavior in Different Settings

Grade Level: _____ Setting: Classroom   Playground   Lunchroom   Other _____
Time: _____

	Child 1	Child 2	Child 3	Child 4	Child 5
Gender:	M F	M F	M F	M F	M F

Social Behavior Categories:

Unoccupied

Onlooker

Conversation
(specify: adult or child)

Play (specify: Solitary,
Parallel, or Group)

   Sensorimotor

   Exploratory

   Constructive

   Dramatic

   Games-with-Rules

   Rough and Tumble

Aggression

Prosocial (helping,
sharing–nonacademic)

Tutor (assist with
academic work)

Other (describe)

Record Form 5.13: Observation of Student Engagement

Time and Setting: _____

Activity/Task Description: _____

	On-Task & Engaged	On-Task, *Not* Engaged	Off-Task, *Not* Disruptive	Off-Task & Disruptive	Other: Describe
Child 1					
Child 2					
Child 3					
Child 4					
Child 5					
Total minutes					

Record Form 5.14: Classroom Environment Survey

Child Choice/Initiative

Children choose tasks from a variety of options, challenge levels.

Children choose who they want to work with.

Children choose how and where to conduct various tasks.

Children can work at their own pace.

Children can determine when they have completed a task or assignment.

Participation

Teacher encourages children to ask questions rather than listen passively.

Most children participate in class discussions.

Most children participate actively in class activities (i.e., appear engaged in tasks).

Affiliation/Cooperation

Children help each other, share materials.

Children appear to know their classmates well.

Children appear to enjoy working together.

Peer assistance (help) with tasks is encouraged.

Competition Emphasis

Children compete for teacher recognition.

Children compete for grades, rewards, or positive evaluation signs (e.g., stars on papers).

Children compete for peer recognition.

Inquiry Focus

Children find out answers to questions through own investigations.

Teacher emphasizes thinking skills and processes of inquiry.

Teacher provides clues, hints, examples to encourage problem-solving.

Teacher encourages creative or novel ideas.

Performance/Evaluation Emphasis

Individual student performance is salient (e.g., grades, "correct" and "incorrect" answers are publicized).

Teacher emphasizes comparison of student performance and behavior.

Praise and other rewards are given mainly to high achievers.

Classroom Management

There appears to be a clear set of rules for students to follow.

Teacher deals consistently with students who break rules.

Children appear to understand what they are expected to do.

Most children demonstrate positive behavior.

(continued on following page)

(continued from previous page)

Teacher Support

The teacher takes a personal interest in the students.

The teacher listens to and respects each child's point of view.

Teacher appears to have high expectations for all students to perform and behave.

Teacher attends appropriately to all students, not just a few.

Teacher appears to accept and be responsive to individual differences in students.

Classroom Materials/Displays

A variety of materials are available for children's use.

Displays show a variety of children's work .

Teacher Structure of Academic Tasks

There is evidence of modifications of academic tasks for individual or small groups of students.

Teacher presents instructional activities materials in a variety of forms (e.g., demonstration, discussion, brief lecture).

Teacher adjusts challenge level of tasks for individual students.

General Classroom Atmosphere

Children appear comfortable, relaxed (few appear tense or nervous).

Classroom atmosphere is *not* characterized by silence, tentative responding by children.

Classroom atmosphere is characterized by cheerful voices of children.